Bordering and Ordering
the Twenty-first Century

HUMAN GEOGRAPHY IN THE NEW MILLENNIUM
ISSUES AND APPLICATIONS

Series Editor
Barney Warf, Florida State University

Human geography is increasingly focused on real-world problems. Applying geographic concepts to current global concerns, this series focuses on the urgent issues confronting us as we move into the new century. Designed for university-level geography and related multidisciplinary courses such as area studies, global issues, and development, these textbooks are richly illustrated and include suggestions for linking to related Internet resources. The series aims to help students to better understand, integrate, and apply common themes and linkages in the social and physical sciences and in the humanities, and, by doing so, to become more effective problem solvers in the challenging world they will face.

Titles in the Series

Boundaries of Faith: Geographical Perspectives on Religious Fundamentalism
Roger W. Stump

Six Billion Plus: Population Issues in the Twenty-first Century
K. Bruce Newbold

Popular Culture, Geopolitics, and Identity
Jason Dittmer

Bordering and Ordering the Twenty-first Century: Understanding Borders
Gabriel Popescu

Bordering and Ordering the Twenty-first Century

Understanding Borders

Gabriel Popescu

ROWMAN & LITTLEFIELD PUBLISHERS, INC.
Lanham • Boulder • New York • Toronto • Plymouth, UK

Published by Rowman & Littlefield Publishers, Inc.
A wholly owned subsidiary of The Rowman & Littlefield Publishing Group, Inc.
4501 Forbes Boulevard, Suite 200, Lanham, Maryland 20706
http://www.rowmanlittlefield.com

Estover Road, Plymouth PL6 7PY, United Kingdom

British Library Cataloguing in Publication Information Available

Library of Congress Cataloging-in-Publication Data

Popescu, Gabriel, 1971–
   Bordering and ordering the twenty-first century : understanding borders / Gabriel Popescu.
      p. cm. — (Human geography in the new millennium : issues and applications)
   Includes bibliographical references and index.
   ISBN 978-0-7425-5621-8 (cloth : alk. paper) — ISBN 978-0-7425-5622-5 (pbk. : alk. paper) — ISBN 978-1-4422-1325-8 (electronic)
   1. Borderlands. 2. Boundaries. 3. Human geography. 4. Political geography. I. Title.
   JC323.P67 2012
   320.1'2—dc23

                              2011022753

∞™ The paper used in this publication meets the minimum requirements of American National Standard for Information Sciences—Permanence of Paper for Printed Library Materials, ANSI/NISO Z39.48-1992.

Printed in the United States of America

To Jodi and Derek

Contents

Preface and Acknowledgments

During the summer of 1989, I was attending summer camp in northern Romania near its border with the late USSR. One day, while on a field trip, we reached the location of the state border. It was a narrow, shallow river, and on the other side we could see a road, a couple of houses, and a few cars passing by. Eastern Europe was under communist rule at that time. Romania endured oppressive rule under the dictatorship of Nicolae Ceauşescu. Few people had passports, and traveling abroad, while not technically illegal, was strongly discouraged and was seen as suspicious by an increasingly paranoid regime that governed its people through fear. Romania was a prison at the time, and its borders were the walls.

The border scene appeared surreal to me, a high school student at the time. The scenery was inviting. There was no sign of the physical disruption that is usually associated with border landscapes. There were no border fences or watchtowers anywhere in sight, just a sunny, forested landscape, with a gurgling creek and a winding road. I felt a strong urge to cross to the other side of the river to a forbidden, unknown place. Then it crossed my mind that this would mean escaping to freedom. For years, I had listened to clandestine radio broadcasts from Western Europe extolling the virtues of capitalism and democracy, and how these countries were welcoming defectors from the communist camp with open arms. However, I could not bring myself to cross the river. Truth be told, there was no point in escaping to the USSR—there was communism there too. I would have been handed back to the Romanian authorities. But this is not the point of the story. I could not cross because I knew it was a border, and crossing it might have had unwanted consequences for the rest of my life. There was no barrier in the middle of the water. The border was all in my mind.

By the end of that year, both Ceauşescu and communism were history in Romania. The walls of the prison tumbled down overnight. There I was, free to roam the globe at last. I quickly used my newly gained political freedom to get a passport and started to travel, taking my revenge on borders, so to speak. In a short time, I traveled in Europe from Turkey and the former Yugoslavia in the south to Poland in the north. However, when I wanted to head farther west into Europe, I found with surprise that it was not that easy for me to gain entry to the West. I first needed a visa, which was difficult to obtain because its requirements largely disqualified someone like me, an undergraduate student interested in backpacking, not in traveling with an organized tour with a predetermined itinerary and expensive hotel. Suddenly I found myself on the wrong side of the border again, with a geographical twist though; this time I was trying to cross in, not to cross out.

This is how I found out that, for me, the borders of France and Germany were not where I knew them to be, but in and around well-guarded embassy buildings in downtown Bucharest. I also learned that these borders were not so formidable after all. Around these buildings, I was approached to pay hefty prices for Western visas if I really wanted so badly to travel there. That is, I could have crossed these telescopic borders if I were willing to bribe the embassy employees in these buildings. This made little sense to me. Why would I pay thousands of dollars for a visa when I was going there to spend my own meager student money? What did make sense, though, was that whoever was willing to pay a bribe worth thousands of dollars to get a visa would not go to France or Germany for tourism. They would go there to stay and send money back any way they could. And so it has become clear to me what a poor fix borders make for systemic issues whose origins lie elsewhere in the world system.

Much has changed since the early 1990s. I eventually traveled extensively in Western Europe and then moved across the ocean to the United States, from where I continued to cross borders regularly, both in my private and professional life. The citizens of my new country enjoy the luxury of crossing most borders visa free. My birth country has joined the European Union, and its citizens can now easily travel throughout much of the world as well. My border story is by no means either unique or the most powerful. There are millions of other stories out there that can teach us much about borders. However, this story reminds me that much has not changed in the world for millions of others. The borders that once excluded me are now to be found elsewhere, in the streets of Moscow, Mexico City, Lagos, and Beijing, to name a few.

I wrote this book with the many others in mind, those who cannot take border crossing for granted because of the geographical assignment the lottery of their birth has dealt them. I also thought of those who have this right but are in danger of losing it in the future because they do not understand it well enough to fight for it.

ACKNOWLEDGMENTS

Throughout the years many people have helped shape my ideas about the issues addressed in this book. I consider myself very fortunate that our paths have crossed and I wish to extend my sincerest gratitude to all of them, especially to Jim Tyner, Jonathan Leib, Barney Warf, and Vasile Cucu, among so many others. I am extremely indebted to a number of people such as Barney Warf and Anne-Laure Amilhat-Szary, who have read the entire manuscript on short notice and have given valuable advice and feedback, as well as to Darren Purcell and Shannon O'Lear, who have read and commented on parts of this book. I am particularly grateful to my long-time friend Cristina Scarlat, who produced much of the cartography in this book even as she was caring for her newborn. My gratitude also goes to James Sidaway for his help with obtaining figure 3.1 and to Jussi Laine for contributing figure 4.2. Susan McEachern at Rowman & Littlefield deserves special thanks for her limitless patience with my repeated deadline offenses and for her constant support of this project from the beginning. Thanks are also due to my colleagues in the Department of Political Science at Indiana University South Bend for providing a remarkably supportive environment in which to write this book. An Indiana University South Bend Faculty Research Grant also provided partial support for this project. The greatest debt I owe is to my family. My wife, Jodi, and my son, Derek, have had to deal with less glamorous parts of the book writing that included long hours at the office and absentmindedness at home. Their support, understanding, and encouragement have been essential to completing this work.

Gabriel Popescu
South Bend, Indiana

Introduction

Browsing through the pages of a world atlas, watching the nightly newscasts, or walking inside government offices, multinational corporations, and classrooms, one will notice that the most common map is the one where the earth's surface is divided by irregular lines called borders or boundaries. This map signifies our taken-for-granted view of the earth's surface. Now take a look at the map as seen from outer space. Borders are nowhere to be found on this map; the natural condition of the earth is borderless. The two maps hardly resemble each other, although they represent the same space. The first is a representation of the earth as we imagine it to be. The second is a representation of the earth as we observe it to be. Nevertheless, only one of these two representations—the one showing the territorial borders of two hundred or so states—became the conventional map of the world, the one with which the majority of people are most familiar. This contradiction offers a useful doorway into the exploration of border spaces.

At the dawn of the twenty-first century, we live divided along cultural, economic, political, and social lines, in a world of territorial borders whose main purpose is to mark differences in space. Our lives have long been spatially ordered by a nested hierarchy of territorial borders—neighborhood, city, county, region, state, and more recently suprastate borders—each with various degrees of visibility in the cultural and physical landscapes. At the same time, we also live in a world defined by mobility that necessitates constant border crossing. Paradoxically, we have been busy surrounding ourselves with borders at one time only to realize that we have to cross them at another time. Contemporary patterns of spatial interaction are creating a complex web of relationships that crisscross the fixed geography of nested borders, further complicating the relationship between borders and society. Today, our lives are spatially ordered by a maze of borders that often have no clear or stable territorial hierarchy. The result is that we have to negotiate more borders in more places and of more kinds than ever before.

State borders are arguably the best known territorial borders. For the most part, their raison d'être is taken for granted in daily life. They are seen as undisputed facts and thus are rarely questioned or challenged. Even when they are challenged, it is often to erect new borders rather than to remove them altogether. Moreover, instances in which borders have been removed reveal that many people have difficulty learning how to live without them. Patterns of social interaction in space leave lasting memories, and borders are only slowly erased from people's mental maps. Thus borders are ubiquitous fixtures in contemporary societies.

The study of borders constitutes a prism through which to examine how contemporary social, cultural, economic, and political processes impact our lives. Most people living outside border areas perceive borders as remote limits of the state, with little direct effect on their livelihoods. Yet state borders play central roles in peoples' lives irrespective of their geographical location. They reach deep into the very fabric of societies, structuring and regulating daily routines as well as long-term aspirations. Borders are the thread connecting apparently unrelated phenomena such as international trade agreements and the outsourcing of jobs, carbon dioxide emissions in industrialized countries and loss of farmland in tropical areas, uneven global development and international migrations, transnational corporations and large-scale recalls of tainted food supplies, transnational terrorism and the scaling back of democracy, consumer habits and resource wars, and deforestation in Amazonia and climate change. In some situations, borders can literally make a life-or-death difference for millions of people, such as between ethnic extermination and peaceful cohabitation, between mass starvation and abundant food supplies, and between economic opportunity and dire poverty. Understanding the dynamic of borders and the bordering processes that produce them is essential.

Recently, borders have taken on heightened significance in an era of globalization. They are central to the profound changes globalization is generating in the way people and societies relate to space at the outset of the twenty-first century. If during the early 1990s globalization pressures on state borders led some to envision the emergence of a borderless world (*debordering*), by the early 2000s it became clear that borders were retaining their significance, albeit under new appearances (*rebordering*). Despite unprecedented opening up to various globalization flows, borders are far from fading away. Instead, they are undertaking both a qualitative and a quantitative transformation by changing their nature and multiplying in number. They are losing some of their territorially linear aspects while acquiring more regional and networklike characteristics. Simultaneously, bordering practices are increasingly reliant on electronic technologies and are becoming embedded into our own bodies through the use of biometric measurements. Border control has been unsettled as well, as more and more authority is transferred from public to private and quasi-public institutions. The outcome is that borders have become intrinsic to everyday life, affecting people and places in a highly unequal manner.

The attacks of September 11, 2001, on the World Trade Center towers in New York City constitute a milestone for the redefinition of borders in the twenty-first century. This was a moment in time and a landmark in space that brought borders to prominence on the mental maps of many ordinary citizens with livelihoods far removed from the daily realities of border life. In the aftermath of that day's events, and with the image of the wrecked place where the towers came to rest etched in people's minds, state borders throughout the world have been entrusted with a new long-term rationale of being the guarantors of our security in a globalizing world characterized by increased cross-border mobility of people, capital, goods, diseases, and ideas. In other words, borders now have to allow mobility while simultaneously protecting against its side effects. The way this challenge is addressed will affect the lives of billions of people around the world and make the difference between war and peace, between oppression and opportunity. Such broad tasks trusted upon borders assures that in the decades to come they will remain central to debates over the nature and shape of social relations.

Therefore it is not surprising that during the last two decades we have witnessed an unprecedented surge of interest in borders. The number of academic works having borders as the center of inquiry has soared, border-focused research centers and institutes have proliferated in many parts of the world, funding for border research has increased, and the media has regularly brought up border-related issues for popular consumption. Such concerted, multidisciplinary endeavors to address the problematic issue of borders have significantly furthered our knowledge of the ways bordering processes work. Nonetheless, we are still far away from a comprehensive understanding of the nature and the direction of contemporary border changes.

The primary aim of this book is to offer a critical understanding of state borders at the beginning of the twenty-first century. My intention here is to go beyond border-making descriptions and problematize borders in order to help readers uncover the inherent complexities they involve, their unfinished character, and their fundamentally contested nature. While state borders make up the book's substance, its spirit seeks to inform discussion about the broader spaces of borders. Rather than assuming that they are a mere attribute of the state, borders are approached as a distinct spatial category that develops in relation to a multitude of social processes and institutions. Throughout this work, the analysis relies on a range of disciplinary insights including geography, international relations, sociology, anthropology, history, political economy, and security studies to explore border-making concepts, processes, discourses, and contexts from a spatial perspective meant to underscore the connections between borders and space. The book combines theoretical perspectives with empirical accounts to discuss how current world issues and events relate to borders, and to address questions that can help readers make better sense of the significance of borders for social life: Why and how have state borders emerged? How have they assumed a certain territorial shape and not others? Who makes borders and how? Who benefits from their making and how? What trends in the development of borders are we witnessing, and, most important, how are they affecting societies?

The wide scope of the argument presented in this book calls for a methodological approach that leaves little room for the detailed treatment of the numerous topics under consideration. I am hopeful the reader will find this trade-off worthwhile. Deciding what to bring in and what to leave out of this volume has proved to be a real challenge. The literature on border studies is so vast and diverse that covering it all would be futile. The spatial perspective adopted here has pushed aside some avenues of inquiry by default, thus providing one way to sort out this literature. My own limitations have played another filtering role that is responsible for additional omissions. Keeping a balance of representation between the world's major regions has been a different challenge. Despite my best efforts to draw on border-making processes and issues in all major regions, Europe and North America remain overrepresented.

The chapters in this book are arranged thematically. Each is structured in two major parts, except chapters 2 and 3, which include several parts. Chapter 1 introduces readers to the study of borders. It begins by discussing the concept of borders together with several other major concepts that are directly related to borders and border making, such as territory and territoriality, nations and nation-states, and sovereignty. These are followed by an examination of the main theoretical contributions to border studies over time and by a synthesis of the current conceptualizations that stress the socially constructed nature of state borders. Chapter 2 summarizes the development of border thinking and making from antiquity to the nation-state era while emphasizing the transition from pre-nation-state zonal frontiers to the present territorially linear borders. Next, the analysis shows how linear state borders have achieved global reach via

European colonialism and identifies a series of key twentieth-century contexts that have produced the current grid of borders that organizes Earth's space.

The question of borders in the globalization era is addressed in chapter 3. The chapter examines how global economic flows, environmental issues, the international human rights regime, and transnational terrorism, among other factors, challenge the territorial nature of state borders and their role of regulating interaction in space. The encounter between globalization flows and state border lines triggers multifaceted processes of change whose purpose is to keep borders relevant in the twenty-first century. Chapter 4 discusses how these dynamics of change are producing globalization's new border spaces. The first section analyzes the interrelated processes of de- and reterritorialization and de- and rebordering that help produce the contemporary border spaces. Simultaneously, this section emphasizes how border permeability is redefined today in the circumstances in which borders are selectively decreasing their role as barriers for certain categories of goods, capital, people, and ideas, while enhancing their barrier role for others. The second section deals with the outcomes that these processes generate, documenting how borders are becoming more diversified and dispersed throughout society, rather than fixed at the outer edges of states. This new geography of globalization's borders incorporates three main types of border spaces: borderlands, border lines, and networked borders.

Chapter 5 looks into the connections between borders and mobility from the perspective of power relationships in society. The first part shows how aspects of transnational mobility such as migration, economic flows, and terrorism have been constructed as major societal security risks to be managed with the help of borders. This view casts mobility and security in antagonistic terms and has led to the reinforcement of the control aspect of borders. The result is the privatization of numerous border functions, as well as their territorial penetration deep into the spaces of everyday life. The second part discusses how seeing borders as tools to control mobile risks works to embed borders in the human body. The body has become the ultimate mobile border that can allow the control of movement at the smallest spatial scale with the help of state-of-the-art technologies such as biometrics and radio frequency identification (RFID) tags. The chapter concludes by examining the implications these novel bordering practices have for the prospects of democratic life in the twenty-first century.

Border-bridging processes that seek to enhance the permeability of borders are the subject of chapter 6. Cross-border cooperation in particular has emerged as a common strategy used to transcend the barrier function of borders through the integration of neighboring borderlands at the subnational level. This process often leads to the formation of cross-border regions that straddle state borders and signal changes in border territoriality. Several examples of cross-border cooperation, including Europe, North and South America, Southeast Asia, Africa, and the Middle East, illustrate the unevenness of cross-border region building across the world. The last part of the chapter discusses a series of directions of border changes in Europe that reflect the possibilities and the limitations of border bridging in cross-border regions with regard to the territorial reorganization of social relations across borders. A short conclusion summarizes the significance of the concept of borders to the organization of social life in the twenty-first century.

1

Making Sense of Borders

INTRODUCING BORDERS

Borders are typically understood as limits and conceived of as lines. They also carry with them a sense of division or separation in space. However, such perceptions offer limited insight into the immensely complex world of borders and boundaries. Border making, also referred to as bordering, is a much more ambiguous process than generally assumed. Nature does not offer compelling rationales to justify the erection of borders between places. Regardless, border making is an old human practice traceable to the earliest societies. This fact indicates that borders are enduring fixtures in human societies, which in turn causes border making to appear as a natural preoccupation for humans (Agnew 2007; Grosby 1995).

The view I've adopted throughout this book is that borders are social phenomena, made by humans to help them organize their lives. Humans erect borders as a way to mediate between the familiar of *here* and the unfamiliar of *there*. Throughout history, border change has been the norm rather than the exception. The meaning of borders has varied widely from place to place as well as from time to time. Borders did not exist in the same location since primordial time, nor did they perform the same functions in all places at all times. Borders are not fixed; they are transitory, and they always change in space and in time. They are not simply lines, but rather areas and networks of variable depth. Borders come in a variety of sizes and shapes, which indicates that they can be constructed based on a multitude of criteria. Thus, all boundaries are made by someone, since individuals define the criteria by which borders are constructed. There are no natural borders to separate human beings in space.

Borders are first and foremost about power. Border making is a power strategy that uses difference to assert control over space by inscribing difference in space. Through borders, difference acquires a territorial expression. The territorialization of difference is an exclusionary power practice with profound structuring effects on societies as it determines membership in society: who belongs where, who is an insider and who is an outsider, who is part of us and who is part of them (Paasi 1996; Sack 1986). Under these circumstances, borders have traditionally served the role of ordering society. Making borders is a means for organizing human behavior in space by regulating movement in space. Thus, bordering space is a means of ordering space (Albert et al. 2001; van Houtum and van Naerssen 2002), two sides of the process by which humans appropriate space.

Some borders are primarily symbolic, cultural, or social in nature, such as linguistic and religious boundaries, or class boundaries. Humans tend to carry such boundaries with them when they move through space. Other borders are primarily physical or territorial in nature, such as state borders. These borders are often well marked on the ground to assure their visibility and stability in the landscape. Most often boundaries are both symbolic and physical at the same time, since symbolic borders can have territorial dimensions, and territorial borders can be symbolic as well. For example, linguistic criteria have been used to establish the location of state borders, while in other instances state borders mark the spatial limits of a language.

With the increase in the number of territorial states throughout the world during the modern era, state borders emerged as the quintessential illustration of borders in people's minds. Although state territorial borders are but one among a large variety of borders, albeit a very significant one, they came to assimilate all other kinds of borders and boundaries to the point that borders are typically understood above all as the geographical limits of the state.

However, state territorial borders should not be understood as the sum of all other borders and boundaries, or as the most important boundaries affecting peoples' lives. Gender, religious, or class boundaries, to mention only a few examples, transcend the simplistic inside/outside divide that state borders have established: they predate even the earliest state borders in antiquity, and they have never fit the territorial matrix of modern state borders. Rather, state borders are best understood as both similar to and dissimilar from other categories of borders. They influence and are influenced by other types of borders and boundaries. Making sense of state borders is part of understanding the central role that all borders and boundaries play in the spatial organization of modern societies.

State borders are political-territorial boundaries. They are territorial and symbolic at the same time, marking the limits of politically organized spaces, as well as suggesting a purported cohesiveness of these spaces (Newman and Paasi 1998). For example, the borders of France represent the limits of the territory of France, and they imply that the people living in this territory are significantly alike. However, the reality is more complex. In addition to the territory of France in Europe, the French state includes several overseas territories stretching from the Pacific Ocean to South America that most people often overlook when thinking about the borders of France (see figure 1.1). At the same time, people inhabiting the territory of France are not necessarily alike, as many natives of French Guyana or New Caledonia hardly identify their group as French.

State borders have the capacity to define the territory they enclose by ascribing it with meaning, while at the same time they are defined by their content by acquiring meaning from what they enclose (Anderson and O'Dowd 1999; Paasi 1996). For example, goods produced inside the borders of the United States are labeled "made in the USA" although they may have been made using parts imported from other countries or may have been made by illegal immigrants. At the same time, the material wealth of the United States suggests to immigrants crossing the U.S. border that they are crossing a gateway to a better life, yet not all Americans are wealthy, and a significant portion of U.S. wealth is generated overseas.

An essential aspect of state borders is their double meaning as lines of separation and contact in space. Whenever a line is drawn between two groups of people, that line acquires two meanings simultaneously. On the one hand it separates the two groups, while on the other it brings them into mutual contact. The double meaning of borders intensifies the complexity of bordering processes. It is impossible to address only one aspect of borders without considering the other one. Every time a border is erected to keep people apart, there will always be some that will want to cross it if for no other reason than because a border exists (Newman 2006b). This phenomenon explains in large part the challenge of tackling complex twenty-first-century issues such as security and immigration at the state's borders.

State borders both separate and bring into contact different national political, economic, and social systems. The managing of state borders across the world is codified in a variety of *border regimes* that range from entirely closed, as in the case of North Korea, where movement and exchange with South Korea is virtually absent, to quite open, as in the case of the internal borders of the European Union, where border control checkpoints have been removed. State borders can be walled fortresses and spaces of Othering one's neighbors, intended to keep insiders in

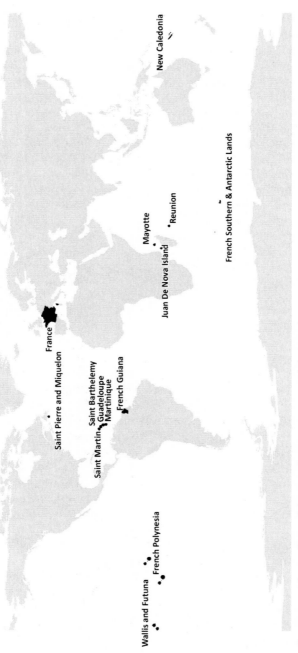

Figure 1.1   The territory of the French state. *Source:* Cristina Scarlat.

and outsiders out, or they can be windows to the world and interfaces of interaction with neighboring countries (Anderson and O'Dowd 1999; Newman and Paasi 1998). However, it is essential to avoid understanding the separation and contact functions of borders as a simplistic binary in which they operate in opposition to each other, as these functions occur simultaneously. In practice, state borders have various degrees of permeability, allowing some types of movement while restricting others. For example, despite the closed border between North and South Korea, there is South Korean cross-border investment in North Korea as well as occasional visits of North Korean delegations to South Korea.

This succinct examination of borders and boundaries illustrates the multifaceted nature of the relationship between bordering processes, space, and society. There is no single meaning or purpose behind state borders. Borders and societies are mutually constitutive processes. People decide to set and maintain territorial borders to divide society, while at the same time territorial borders have the power to shape our lives, sense of identity, and how we think about our neighbors. Understanding this symbiotic relationship constitutes the starting point in making sense of the role and the functions of borders in the twenty-first century, as well as in facilitating public involvement toward making border spaces more democratic and more inclusive of the interests of all categories of citizens irrespective of their status in society, ethnic identity, or national belonging.

Borders and Territory

Boundaries and territory are intrinsically connected concepts. Today, the most widely accepted definition of a border is that of dividing two territorial entities, or that of marking the limit of a territorial entity (Newman 2003). Borders can thus be regarded as lines of separation and contact not only between human groups but between territories as well.

Generally, the term *territory* refers to a portion of space that is claimed or occupied by a person, a group of people, or an institution (Paasi 2003b). In a physical sense, space exists without borders or delineations. The term "space" can be applied to the entire surface of the earth. However, people would not be able to make practical sense of space without the existence of borders to delineate it. Borders are discontinuities in space that render space meaningful by compartmentalizing it into distinctive units. Territory as a portion of space implies the existence of boundaries: a territory is a bounded space (Gottmann 1973). The notion of borders is intrinsic to any understanding of territory since we cannot conceive of a portion of space without conceiving of its limits in regard to other portions of space. In this sense, borders produce territory; they are constitutive of territory.

People relate to territory through territoriality. Territoriality is the process whereby individuals or groups lay claim to territory. According to Sack (1986, 1), territoriality is "a spatial strategy to affect, influence, and control resources and people, by controlling area." Territories are defended and contested against others through territoriality. Therefore, territoriality can be understood as a form of power over space (Sack 1986). However, control over a territory is typically asserted by the imposition of borders that are used to regulate access to the territory. The erection of borders around territories emerges as a crucial moment in appropriating space; thus it is a political strategy used to secure power in society (Storey 2001).

The most pervasive form of territoriality today is political territoriality, meaning that most political power in society is organized territorially through bounded portions of space. Territory is important for political governance because it provides a locus for the exercise of political authority over a range of interests. Location inside the borders of a territory defines membership to a group, instead of, for example, kinship relationships or similarity of interests among the members of the group. Hunting-and-gathering societies, for example, while employing territoriality for purposes such as delimiting and defending land, rarely used rigid territorial borders to define belonging to a community. Instead, these societies had a social definition of territoriality and of borders that was based primarily on kinship relations. Modern societies, however, have a territorial definition of society, using territoriality and borders for a wide range of purposes in order to define social membership (Soja 1971).

Borders and the State

Political territoriality is most strongly manifested today in the form of the modern state. The state is generally associated with political power within territorial borders (Kazancigil 1986). According to Paasi (1996), in an empirical context the state is a specific territory with recognized borders, whereas in a theoretical context the state is a set of institutions aimed at producing and reproducing society. Thus, as a political institution that possesses territorial power, the state has an area over which it claims jurisdiction, and borders that control mobility. Today, the national state has come to represent the basic division of political space. The entire landmass of the world is parceled into roughly two hundred neatly delineated states.

States are historically dynamic artifacts. They are not universal or natural political-territorial institutions for the organization of society. Tribes, which have served in many cultures to organize society, long preceded the state. Moreover, states are not permanent. They frequently appear and disappear from the world political map. The Polish state disappeared three times in the course of its history; Texas was an independent state before its incorporation into the United States, and South Sudan is the latest state to appear in the world in 2011 by breaking off from Sudan. These examples imply that the borders of these states underwent considerable changes as well. Also, states are not fixed. They constantly change their territorial shape. The vast majority of states existing today established their current borders only in the past fifty years.

Throughout history there have been several types of state, such as city-states, empires, and nation-states. Each type relates in different ways to borders to delineate its political territoriality. The walls of the city-states of antiquity and the medieval era did not delineate political borders, since these cities also incorporated the surrounding hinterland. City-state walls performed primarily a defensive purpose. Empires were often composed of discontinuous territories, and their borders were generally unmarked. Nation-states, on the other hand, tend to have well-delineated territories and clearly marked borders.

The nation-state is the contemporary type of state that emerged approximately two hundred years ago in the wake of the French Revolution in 1789. A nation-state is understood as a country inhabited by a group of people who see themselves as one distinct community (Paasi 1996). Its distinctiveness consists mainly in the conceptual merging of political territoriality, as expressed in the institution of the state, with ethnic and cultural identity, as expressed in the idea of the nation, so that their boundaries coincide. A nation is typically defined as a group of people who imagine sharing common elements such as language, history, ethnic background, political institutions, and attachment to a particular territory (B. Anderson 1991). However, there is little agreement as to what exactly the proportion of the mix should be, who decides when a group of people reaches the status of a nation, and where to establish the borders of a nation. As a result of these dilemmas, the number of nations in the world varies widely from several hundred to several thousand. The number of states, however, is just under two hundred.

The main predicament of the idea of the nation-state—one state, one nation—is that it assumes congruence between the territorial borders of the state and group identity (Knight 1982). As there are many more nations than there are states, the nation-state appears a theoretical impossibility. Instead of seeking to delink the ideas of statehood and nationhood, during the last two hundred years state governments throughout the world have been actively involved in a process of nation building using the ideology of nationalism. Nationalism is a territorial ideology that seeks to bind the nation and the state by creating identity based on bounded space (A. Murphy 1996). The erection of borders behind which to build homogenous nations has been a key feature of nationalism (Agnew 2007). At its best, nationalism allows the emancipation of certain groups of people from the domination of tyrannical rulers. At its worst, nationalism is responsible for outright forms of violence as demonstrated by the 1990s' ethnic cleansing in both the former Yugoslavia and USSR, to mention only two examples.

Gradually, the nation-state circumscribed social relations inside its borders to an unprecedented extent. It became normal to imagine all the citizens of a given state forming one national society that was distinct from the ones beyond the borders with the neighboring states. Under these circumstances, the nation-state came to be seen as a container of society (Taylor 1994), with the borders of the state forming the walls of the container. Borders became major tools for regulating social relations both inside the container and across containers. However, nation building did not result in absolute control over the society contained by the state borders. The intensification of transnational flows of capital and people challenges the nation-state's monopoly of power inside its borders and suggests the erosion of the power of borders to serve as territorial containers.

Borders and Sovereignty

The principle of sovereignty constitutes the linchpin between territories, states, and borders. Sovereignty is the claim of exclusive power over a territory. A state's claims to the monopoly of power within its territorial borders have been codified in the modern principle of territorial sovereignty (Gottmann 1973). Although this situation has always been more of an aspiration than an accomplishment, these persistent claims of sovereign control within one's own borders have led to widespread association of sovereignty with bordered territoriality (Agnew 2009).

During the medieval era, sovereignty was invested in the person of the monarch and signified the divine authority of the emperor to rule over his or her subjects regardless of the territorial borders of the empire. With the advent of the modern territorial state during the seventeenth century, however, sovereignty was gradually transferred from the person of the monarch to the territory of the state (A. Murphy 1996; Taylor and Flint 2000). The divine element was replaced by the popular will of the people, at least in theory. A person's political status changed from being a subject of a ruler to being a citizen of a state. The borders of a state came to determine one's political belonging.

Borders are linked to sovereignty because they mark the formal extension of the territorial power of the state. In legal terms, borders demarcate states' sovereignty. The territorial sovereignty of one state starts at its borders and ends at its borders. Put differently, the same state border signifies the end of the authority of one state and the beginning of another's. Consequently, sovereignty is a territorially exclusive practice. A state's legal and taxation systems, social protection policies, and police jurisdiction, for example, all end at its borders, only to reemerge on the other side of the border as another state's practices and policies.

In the modern world, sovereignty has a dual aspect: it is both inward looking and outward looking. This dual status implies that the power of a state within its territorial borders cannot be challenged by other states, while at the same time, for this situation to be possible, states must mutually recognize each other's sovereignty over a bounded territory (Giddens 1987; Wallerstein 1999). Under these circumstances, territorial sovereignty has become the fundamental principle of organization of international relations. It is not sufficient for a state to declare its sovereignty within specific territorial borders, but these borders have to also be recognized by other states as well. The principle of territorial sovereignty has created an interstate system in which states are assumed to be equal. The stability of the system is derived from the fact that every state has to recognize and to respect other states' territorial sovereignty. In practice, however, this has hardly been the case (Agnew 2009). Throughout the world, states have frequently infringed on each other's sovereignty by advancing territorial claims against their neighbors or demanding border adjustments. Nonetheless, the principle of territorial sovereignty as such has not been in question (A. Murphy 1999). It is only recently that the globalization of capitalist relations of production as well as of numerous cultural and social processes have introduced considerable pressures for changing the way we make sense of fundamental aspects of state territorial sovereignty.

THINKING BORDERS

During the last two decades there has been a dramatic increase in the border studies literature across a broad range of academic disciplines, such as geography (Kaplan and Hakli 2002; Kolossov and O'Loughlin 1998; Newman 1999; Paasi 1996; Pavlakovich-Kochi et al. 2004; Rumley and Minghi 1991; van Houtum et al. 2005); international relations (Albert et al. 2001; Ruggie 1993; Rumford 2008a); anthropology (Donnan and Wilson 1999; Michaelsen and Johnson 1997; Pellow 1996); political science (Ansell and Di Palma 2004; Brunet-Jailly 2007; M. Anderson 1996); sociology (Delanty 2006; Kearney 1991; O'Dowd and Wilson 1996); history (Martinez 1994; Sahlins 1989); and philosophy (Balibar 2002; Smith 1995), as well as across interdisciplinary boundaries (Anderson et al. 2003; Eskelinen et al. 1999; Ganster and Lorey 2005; Nicol and Townsend-Gault 2005;

Shapiro and Alker 1996). The abundance and diversity of approaches to the understanding of borders resists neat classifications and points to the multi- as well as interdisciplinary nature of recent border studies. However, some scholars notice that a unified theory of borders and bounding processes has failed yet to emerge, while others maintain that borders are unique phenomena that cannot be explained by an overarching theory. Many authors agree that while an overarching theory of borders may not be either necessary or possible, there are a series of common themes in the study of bordering processes (Newman 2006a; Paasi 2009).

This section surveys the main trends and approaches in the multidisciplinary study of boundaries with a focus on the developments taking place in the discipline of geography, where the emphasis on territorial borders has traditionally figured high on the research agenda. The emerging themes do not constitute rigid classifications of border studies as there has been constant borrowing and overlapping between various academic traditions. The goal is to provide a general orientation through the maze of border studies in order to help develop an understanding of the existing scholarship on borders.

Frontiers and Border Lines

In geography, border studies have traditionally been a major subfield of political geography where borders were thought of as the limits of the political organization of territory and as the limits of a state's territorial power (Minghi 1963/1969; Prescott 1987). During the first two decades of the twentieth century, the border studies literature consisted primarily of descriptive case studies that focused on the historical evolution of borders and on their physical features. Two major themes emerged from these early works: the differentiation among concepts such as frontier and border, and the view of borders in natural or artificial terms (e.g., Ancel 1938; Fawcett 1918).

An understanding of state borders as frontiers rather than borders was prevalent at this time. At the core of the issue has been the zonal character of the frontier versus the linear nature of borders. Frontiers are territories with variable spatial depth. Borders are simply territorial lines lacking spatial depth. It is generally accepted that the term *frontier* comes from "front," which suggests contact, and an outward orientation, while the term *boundary* comes from "bounds," which means territorial limits and separation and suggests an inward orientation (Kristof 1959). Frontiers were understood as transition zones, often sparsely populated and remotely situated in relation to surrounding centers of power. They incorporated a significant mixture of populations and cultures, were loosely controlled by their political centers, and provided a gradual transition from one state to another (Prescott 1965). Although some frontiers included defensive walls and border pillars, there were few political border lines running through frontiers. Rather, the entire zone of the frontier constituted the border. From a geopolitical perspective, frontiers were seen as buffer zones that were supposed to absorb or smooth out interstate conflicts. It was common practice for nineteenth-century empires to establish buffer zones between them. Afghanistan, established as a buffer zone between the British and the Russian empires, is among the most notorious examples of such practices. However, the view of state borders as frontiers was later abandoned in favor of the linear concept of borders (Kolossov 2005).

The assumption of "natural borders" of the state dominated early thinking about borders across academic disciplines. Numerous approaches to the study of borders owed much to the organic and environmental deterministic worldviews that were used at the time in the conceptualization of the nation-state. According to Friedrich Ratzel (1897), an influential figure in early political geography, the state was an organism and the border areas formed the epidermis of this organism that both provided protection and allowed exchanges (A. Murphy 1996; Prescott 1987). Ratzel's laws of territorial growth stated that the borders of the larger areas embrace the borders of the smaller ones. In this view, borders are an expression and a measure of state power. The balance of power between countries was dependent on the character of the borders between them.

The appeal of the idea that states must have natural borders is related to the fact that physical landscape features such as rivers, mountain ridges, and seas appear to constitute sharp natural barriers or limits. It was tempting to imagine these landscape features as determining the location of state borders. The "natural borders" thesis implied that states lacking natural borders had to acquire them to enter normality (Agnew 2002). Such a perspective overlooked the fact that landscape features are not necessarily barriers to human activity. Rivers, mountains, and seas everywhere have been traversed by humans since time immemorial, and numerous civilizations have spanned river valleys, mountain ranges, and seas.

Between the 1920s and 1950s the literature on boundaries expanded significantly. The two world wars and the peace treaties in their aftermath that settled new borders provided the impetus for much of this scholarship. Border classifications and typologies were the main preoccupation in border studies in this period. Typical was the analysis of borders at the international scale and the approach to borders as fixed and stable lines that marked sharp differences between neighboring societies. Boundary studies were part of a search for causes of international conflict (Minghi 1963/1969). Boundaries were understood above all as geographical limits of the nation-state, and their existence was taken for granted. As a consequence, many boundary studies were rich in empirical descriptions and saw state borders as natural separations between peoples (Hakli and Kaplan 2002; Newman and Paasi 1998).

Among the most enduring contributions to border studies are border-making typologies developed by Hartshorne (1936) and Jones (1945). Hartshorne differentiated borders after the characteristics of the cultural landscape they passed through. *Antecedent* borders were those established before the settlement of a region. Such borders were thought to determine later patterns of difference between settler societies on each side of the border. *Subsequent* borders were those established after the settlement of an area. They supposedly reflected the already existing ethnic and political patterns of difference. *Superimposed* borders were those imposed by colonial powers without much regard for local patterns of settlement. They were often geometric lines that divided ethnic groups and tribes, mainly in Africa, Asia, and Latin America. *Relict* borders were boundary lines that no longer marked political divisions but that were still visible in the landscape.

Concerned with more practical processes of border making, Jones distinguished four main stages in the establishment of international borders. The *allocation* stage consists in the initial political decision of the interested states to distribute territories between themselves. *Delimitation* consists in the selection of a boundary line to divide territories. *Demarcation* refers to the actual marking of the boundary line on the ground, involving exact measurements, planting border markers, erecting fences, and designating border crossing posts. The *administration* stage involves the establishment of a border regime consisting of rules and regulations for the management of the border.

From the 1950s to the 1980s, boundary studies lost significant momentum. This change is explained by the postwar decline of political geography as a discipline, on the grounds that in its "organic" form it fueled Nazi geopolitics (Newman 2006a). Approaches to interstate borders in this period are often characterized as "functional." Their main thrust was to examine the functions of borders in relation to economic exchange flows (Kolossov 2005). Analyses in terms of an open–closed border continuum indicated the degree of border permeability for various economic processes such as labor migration, investment, or trade. These studies laid the foundations for cross-border administrative cooperation between neighboring states and were aimed at addressing issues of common interest in border areas (Newman 2003). In addition, they introduced a more dynamic view of borders as economic and social phenomena while at the same time directing attention to the impact of local-scale border processes on surrounding regions. Nonetheless, these approaches continued to accept state borders as a given, leaving their theoretical foundation unquestioned.

The main criticism of traditional border studies is related to their primarily descriptive nature and their lack of critical interrogation of the nature of state boundaries. Echoing these remarks, concern has been expressed that the traditional approaches and their methodology produced findings that were in conflict with each other (Minghi 1963/1969). Traditional studies were more concerned with the measurement of borders than with asking critical questions about their nature and meaning, such as why and how they were built in one location and not another, and why they looked and functioned in one way and not the other. If border disputes existed, it was thought that this was because the borders were not delineated well enough, and not because power relations existed between states and between different social groups. State borders and their role in society were conceptualized as determined by states' actions; thus the possibility that the state borders themselves influenced the actions of the state was in large part overlooked.

The Social Construction of Borders

The revitalization of interest in the study of borders after the 1980s can be attributed to challenges and changes unleashed by the contemporary round of globalization. At an empirical level, the creation of many new borders and the dismantling of some of the seemingly well-established ones throughout the 1990s created an impetus for understanding the continued appeal of the practice of making boundaries. At a theoretical level, a discrepancy began to take shape between the vision of a dynamic deterritorialized world of flows focused on mobility and exchange, replacing the static world of places focused on bounded territoriality on the one hand, and the reality of the selective role of borders, allowing flows of capital but stopping flows of labor on the other (Anderson et al. 2003). Given these circumstances, various lines of research in contemporary border studies show how understanding borders in the broader context of territoriality and their role in the production and reproduction of territorial entities contributes to the understanding of how borders are central sites where the international political system is produced (Anderson et al. 2003).

Among the initial approaches that reflected these new realities was Rumley and Minghi's (1991) attempt to overcome the problems of traditional approaches to border landscape studies. They moved away from the focus on the visible functions of border lines to see border landscapes as a product of a set of cultural, economic, and political interactions that occur in space. They called for border studies to take more interest in the symbolic qualities of the border landscapes, emphasizing the importance of the social meanings people attribute to them. They also called for approaches that see border landscapes and their problems from the viewpoint of neighboring states and their inhabitants.

The interest in border landscapes contributed to a change of focus in border studies from interstate border lines to borderlands. The term *borderland* has often been used in early border studies in close association with frontiers and borders. The main difference consists in the fact that borderlands, or border regions, are geographical areas situated along state borders. Interstate borders run through borderlands. Early frontiers had no political border lines running through them. The concept of borderlands poses that a border, because of its influence over the surrounding areas (known as a "border effect"), creates its own distinctive region. As a consequence, a border can serve not only as an element of division in space, but also as a vehicle of creating new territorial realities (Rumley and Minghi 1991). Therefore, in order to make sense of state borders, there is a need to go beyond the preoccupation with border lines themselves and to take into account broader areas—the borderlands—where social processes induced by borders, such as perceptions, stereotypes, and actions, are experienced and reproduced (Michaelsen and Johnson 1997; Newman 2006a; Paasi 1996). Conceptualized this way, borderlands resemble the frontiers of the pre-nation-state era. The two can share common transition zone characteristics, such as a mixture of populations, cultural hybridity, and hybrid economies, that tend to reduce difference. Borderlands, thus, can function as bridges between societies, offering opportunities for cross-border cooperation.

Inspired by the complex cultural, social, and political characteristics of the U.S.-Mexico border, Martinez (1994) developed a typology of borderland development that sheds light on the nature and the range of possibilities of interactions across borderlands. *Alienated* borderlands are representative of hostile circumstances and closed borders between neighboring states. *Coexistent* borderlands indicate a state of mutual ignorance and parallel development of border regions. *Interdependent* borderlands are indicative of cooperative interstate relations, relatively open borders, and complementary border economies. *Integrated* borderlands point to situations where the barrier function of borders has been largely overcome and the entire border region functions as one socioterritorial unit.

In the late 1980s, the social sciences started to incorporate social theory and poststructuralist theories of culture. In border studies, the emphasis was placed on the multidimensional character of social, cultural, and spatial borders and borderlands with the aim of contributing to the debates in social science concerning the meaning and role of difference in society (Bucken-Knapp et al. 2001; Diener and Hagen 2009). These new approaches, drawing on authors like Derrida, Giddens, Said, and later Foucault, Deleuze and Guattari, Agamben, and Balibar, among others, relied on the idea that borders are socially constructed to explore how changing spatial patterns of interaction between people affect the role and the meaning of borders (Berg and van Houtum 2003; Kramsch and Hooper 2004). At the same time, there was an increasing awareness of the role played by language in the social and political construction of state borders. Border studies became increasingly critical of the uncontested nature of borders as ostensibly natural divisions between societies. They highlighted the fact that the process of bordering is essentially political, and that this political dimension permeates border making at all scales, from the daily life of individuals to international relations (Paasi 1996).

These postmodern and poststructuralist approaches found their way into boundary studies in the late 1980s, inducing major breakthroughs in the conceptualization of borders. One of the early insights was the conceptualization of the connection between collective identification (or group identity) and border making, which led to a view of borders as indeterminate, mutable, and socially constructed (Paasi 1999; Pellow 1996; Williams 2003). Borders were considered now to have multiple dimensions and were approached contextually (Newman 1999; Paasi 1999). In the first case, multidimensionality acknowledges that there are numerous facets to borders other than the territorial limits of the state. The presence of a border influences society across a multitude of scales and impacts different people in different ways. In the second case, contextuality means that borders cannot be properly understood outside of the context in which they exist. Borders acquire their roles as barriers or bridges from the context in which they are erected and in which they function.

At the same time, there was a broader preoccupation with the process of bounding in general (Newman 2003; Williams 2003), which led to the idea that even invisible borders matter because they are perceived by people who experience and then reproduce these borders in the form of visible borders (Conversi 1999). Boundaries and borders were approached not only in their visible, physical aspect, but also in terms of their symbolic, less tangible meaning. This transformation led to the understanding that borders mean different things for different people in different circumstances.

What the new approaches to border studies pointed to was the fact that the *processes* of bordering rather than borders themselves were essential for the understanding of border spaces. Borders are never finished; instead they are always in the making, always being imagined and reimagined. What matters more is the border-making process rather than the shape borders assume at one time or another. This shift in thinking led to new questions about borders. Why, how, and by whom are borders erected? Whose interests are served, and whose interests are hurt by the existence of borders? How do borders acquire their meanings in people's minds, and how do people navigate the multiple meanings of borders? Questions such as these inform the quest for a critical understanding of the socially constructed nature of borders.

To illustrate the breadth and depth of the contemporary border studies literature, the following section sketches the main directions of border research since the 1990s. The four broad directions presented here are by no means exhaustive or mutually exclusive. In fact, most of the themes are interrelated.

Discourses, Borders, and Identity

Borders are today largely seen as discursively constructed (Newman and Paasi 1998). In the social sciences, discourses are typically understood as constituted by a collection of theories, writings, public speeches, and popular media broadcasts that create a specific context that dominates the interpretation of a given issue (Tyner 2005). Discourses are inevitably biased representations of reality. The notion that discourses play crucial roles in the construction of borders shows that the existence of borders requires a process of continual discursive production and reproduction in order to maintain borders' relevance in people's lives. Geography and history textbooks, images of border-crossing checkpoints or fences, patriotic songs, national maps, and passport control booths all constitute powerful symbols that serve to perpetuate and reinforce state borders in people's minds.

Borders are not mirrorlike reflections of the divisions existing in the physical-cultural landscape but are fabrications people make to legitimate distinctions between them (Eskelinen et al. 1999; Paasi 1996). Consequently, the production of borders is a geographically and historically contingent process, and therefore the study of borders must be contextual. Paasi (1996, 1999) suggests that the proper context for the study of borders is situated not only in the adjacent borderland areas but also in the continual process of nation building, the process that provides a narrative account for the identity of the nation-state. At the same time, local experiences and narratives of the border also inform bordering discourses and provide the appropriate context for the understanding of borders.

The idea of the discursive creation of borders prepares the ground for the conceptualization of the "'chicken and egg' mutually enforcing relationship" (Newman 2003, 130) between borders and identity, where borders are viewed as identity-constitutive, yet at the same time they can also be erected as a result of discourse-constituted group identity. Drawing on Said's (1978) conceptualization of the role of space in the construction of Otherness, the current literature on borders stresses that the collective territorial identity is not generated naturally but is achieved through the erection of borders by exploiting "us-versus-them" type discourses (Albert et al. 2001; Donnan and Wilson 1999; Paasi 1996).

Paasi (1996) establishes an analytic framework to explain how group identities are constructed through the use of territorial borders. He identifies four discourses:

We/here—employed to suggest integration within the borders of territorial units such as the nation-state.
We/there—demonstrates intention to integrate social groups beyond borders, such as separated minorities.
We/they within a territory—designates refugees and Others inside the borders of a territory.
Other/there—used to inscribe difference on social groups situated outside the borders of a territory.

The implications of these sociospatial discourses for the understanding of phenomena such as nationalism and ethnicity, for example, are paramount. Borders and borderlands emerge as central sites for exploring the construction of various collective identities and of the ways these identities influence and are influenced by the context of the borderland (Bucken-Knapp and Schack 2001).

Borders and Power

Borders are sites of power where different political, economic, and social systems come into contact. Border landscapes with barbed wire, watchtowers, and checkpoints are a very visible aspect of this power (Donnan and Wilson 1999). However, not all power is visible in border landscapes. Borders are present in various cultural and social practices in which power is invisible (Amoore 2006; Paasi 1999; Paasi and Prokkola 2008). Borders may conceal power resulting from political or economical factors that belong to a multitude of scales beyond and below the national scale. In this way, borders appear to be responsible for various issues that affect peoples' lives that in fact arise from the desire of one group to dominate another. Moreover, groups that desire to gain or maintain power over other groups and territories can resort to the erection of borders on the grounds of ethnic or religious difference in order to mask their goals of domination. In order to unearth the power of boundaries, we need to ask whose interests are being served by the imposition and maintaining of various borders.

In contemporary approaches, borders are often understood as mechanisms that render power emerging from human interactions visible. They are expressions of power relations, and they can be perceived as "flows of power" given their dynamic nature (Paasi 1999). Borders embody a variety of contradictions and conflicts that are the result of the arbitrary circumstances of boundary making (Anderson et al. 2003; Newman and Paasi 1998). As a result, understanding borders as sites of power helps us to understand the forces behind various social conflicts, and this in turn can help us to better manage or prevent them.

Borders as Institutions

Underlining this approach is the idea that borders are the institutional outcome of boundary-making processes that shape the surrounding region. The construction of border lines is part of the construction of territorial units in space. It is through the process of institutionalization that territorial units receive their borders that distinguish them from other territories (Paasi 1996, 1999). Borders are found in institutions such as education, mass media, ceremonies, and others. National education in history and geography, for example, serves to preserve the idea of interstate borders.

As institutions, borders perpetuate difference in space. The institutionalization of borders formalizes inclusion and exclusion in society by inscribing difference into law. An individual's identity is stamped in passports and recorded when she or he crosses international borders. Order and control of society are achieved through the regulation of movement across space that is stored into databases at border-crossing checkpoints in order to keep track at all times of one's presence in or absence from his or her designated place.

The institutional approach stresses the multiple and changing meaning of borders in different historic and spatial circumstances. Borders are evolving institutions that acquire their meaning in relation to a host of events taking place at local, national, or global scales (Newman and Paasi 1998). Borders as institutions develop their own history. At one point in time, state borders may be relatively open, such as before World War I; at another they may be relatively closed, such as during the Cold War; and yet at another they may reopen again, such as at the end of the Cold War.

The institutionalization of borders brings about a multiscalar hierarchy of borders. Different levels of government are present in border areas, imposing different jurisdictions on the inhabitants of borderlands. While much attention is paid in general to the all-too-visible state borders, regional and local boundaries, such as administrative or municipal borders, may often have a key importance in the lives of many people (Newman 2003).

Borders and Globalization

Globalization-inspired border studies cover a vast array of topics that raise the question of the future role of state borders confronted by the growing power of a transnational economy and by global cultural influences (Hakli and Kaplan 2002; Newman 2003). Initially, the "borderless-world" thesis has provided an influential account of globalization's impact on state borders (Ohmae 1990). Much of this literature tends to view borders as obsolete barriers affecting the free movement of various global flows, and to assume that in a global world the mobility of social relations will ostensibly replace their territoriality. Consequently, globalization is understood as leading to the deterritorialization of the system of territorially sovereign states, which in turn will lead to the fading away of state borders.

The borderless-world thesis has been vigorously criticized by many geographers on the grounds that it presents a simplistic and idealized vision of globalization (Toal 1999). Far from fading away, it appears that the more territorial borders fall apart, the more various groups around the world cling to place, nation, and religion as markers of their identity (Harvey 1989). In other words, the reduction in capacity of territorial borders to separate and defend against others often elicits adverse reactions in numerous populations. Difference between people and places may be socially constructed through the erection of boundaries, but this does not mean that it is not deeply internalized by the members of a society. So far, the consumption-dominated rhetoric of globalization has done little to uncouple the feeling of difference that borders create from the formation of people's territorial identities.

If the "space of flows" of globalization is to replace the "space of places" of nation-states, this would imply the emergence of a global polity and an end to territorial bordering as a mode of controlling and ordering society. There is little evidence that this process is plausible in the foreseeable future (Anderson et al. 2003; Taylor 1995). In reality, both spaces have coexisted for a long time without one totally replacing the other. If some of the globalization flows deemphasize territorial borders, this does not inevitably entail *deterritorialization* and the disappearance of boundaries (Newman 1999, 2006a). Rather, we are witnessing a *reterritorialization* of political power that includes a selective reduction of the barrier role of state borders for specific categories of flows, as well as a restructuring and reorganization of state territorial sovereignty to include other political organizations beyond the nation-state. The increased mobility of social relations has not displaced their territoriality. Instead, it has modified it. State borders are becoming more complex and differentiated rather than withering away. They exist simultaneously on various spatial scales, in a myriad of practices and discourses included in culture, politics, economics, and education. Borders, thus, remain central to the process of globalization since "they are where the 'space of flows' meet (or collide?) with the 'space of places'" (Anderson et al. 2003, 10).

The ambiguous role of state borders under contemporary globalization is best revealed by the distinction practiced by governments around the world between politics on the one hand and economics on the other. The key argument here is that while national political regulation most often stops at state borders, the seemingly nonpolitical economic activities can easily cross state borders and elude national regulation. This disconnection has been typically dealt with through a circular logic in which borders are seen to cause problems and then new borders are required to fix these problems. For example, governments commonly invoke the territorial limits state borders impose on their capacity to control the adverse effects that certain global flows have on domestic markets, only to attempt to expand these borders into cyberspace as a strategy to address this issue.

Security-related approaches constitute another important perspective on the impact of globalization on borders. In the post-9/11 world, border *securitization* discourses have gained a firm grip on many decision makers' minds. These discourses—in existence before September 11, 2001, as well—see state borders as the ultimate line of defense for societies confronted not only with transnational terrorism but also with migration flows and a variety of other "threats." Overall, border securitization marks a movement toward reinforcing state borders to make them more difficult to cross for certain categories of people. This process is in stark contrast to border-opening processes, and it is most evident in North America and Europe, which previously experienced the greatest degree of border opening (Andreas and Biersteker 2003). The outcome of border securitization is to hinder interaction across borders and to reinforce retrenchment behind the illusory comfort of territorial borders. However, this is not to be understood as a reclosing of borders in the sense of a return to the past. It is difficult to imagine the rigid control of borders as an appropriate answer to issues generated by globalization (Brunet-Jailly 2007). Additional explanations are needed to adequately understand the role of state borders under globalization.

To this end, state borders have recently been likened to filters or firewalls that can control mobility by "purifying" it. Borders are seen as acquiring network characteristics and becoming territorially networked as well as digitized. Behind this approach is a recognition of the fact that borders and border functions are becoming dispersed through society rather than remaining concentrated at the edges (Balibar 2004; Rumford 2006a; Walters 2006a). Border functions that were once performed at border-crossing checkpoints can now take place anywhere inside the territory of a state. In numerous instances, people's identities are screened or prescreened before they even reach the state border, that is, when they apply for visas, for special border passes, or at a bus station when they embark for a border-crossing trip. Biometric identification of people as well as other technology-driven procedures are increasingly becoming common border-crossing experiences. In this way, state borders are becoming more personal in a very real sense. These bordering practices lead to the multiplication of borders in society and to an increase in their complexity. People are now encountering borders in more places and more often than before. In the end, the networking of borders increases their power of ordering people's lives precisely at a time when these lives are becoming more mobile in space due to the time-space compression that accompanies globalization.

2

Borders Before and During the Modern Era

STATE LIMITS IN ANTIQUITY

Frontiers and borders have a long history that can be traced back to antiquity, more than two thousand years ago. Conceptually, at the time there was no difference between the two terms when it came to state limits. However, the precise meaning of state borders in antiquity has long been disputed. At the core of the debate has been the zonal versus the linear nature of state borders. While there is significant consensus that state limits in antiquity closely resembled zonal frontiers, the presence of sharp separation lines such as the walls of ancient empires seem to indicate a close resemblance to contemporary border lines.

Much of the controversy has been sustained by the frequent use of a modern Cartesian spatial perspective to understand ancient borders established at a time when other spatial perspectives predominated (Warf 2008). This has obscured the fact that the modern one-dimensional spatial understanding of the relationship between borders, territory, group identity, and state sovereignty was substantially different before modern times.

The Roman *limes* and the Chinese Great Wall are among the best known borders of antiquity. Also well documented are the bordering practices of ancient Egypt and Persia (Mojtahed-Zadeh 2006). These ancient borders assumed a territorially linear form and were often marked in the landscape by walls or boundary pillars. The northern border of the Roman Empire stretched across Europe from present-day Scotland to Ukraine and consisted of a series of walls and forts that hosted garrisons charged with defending the frontier, maintaining the roads, and levying taxes on commerce. The Chinese Great Wall was an elaborate structure that functioned in much the same way. Ancient Egypt also had territorial borders that were marked by pillars, statues, and inscriptions, a system of forts with garrisons, and even a customs system with customs agents (Goyon 1993). These examples seem to point to little conceptual difference between ancient and modern state border lines.

A deeper analysis of ancient borders reveals that despite apparent similarities, state borders in antiquity differed both in their meaning and in practice from the borders of the modern state. Although the concept of linear borders was known and used in antiquity, it did not assume either a generalized or a continuous practice (Pohl 2001). Walls, pillars, and military installations did not completely surround the ancient states. An ancient empire may have erected protective walls at one frontier only to leave another frontier open, and to use the territory of a subordinate state as a frontier in another part of the empire. Moreover, the famous Roman *limes* and Chinese Great Wall were not continuous structures but were made up of a number of sections interrupted by open spaces. They were also built and rebuilt over many hundreds or even thousands of years, and they often shifted location. For example, today's most impressive segments of the Great Wall are feudal structures built to incorporate older wall segments that existed during antiquity. Several other long walls built during antiquity are located farther north, and they are much more modest structures (Dalin 1984/2005) (see figure 2.1). Evidence shows that ancient borders such as the *limes* and the Great Wall were often easily permeable to trade and other types of exchanges (Whittaker 1994).

These bordering practices suggest that ancient borders had a primarily defensive and commercial meaning. Walls and fortifications were built to function mainly as defense lines to protect against "barbarians" and to control trade, not to mark the sovereignty of the state. At the time, sovereignty was generally conceived as jurisdiction over subjects rather than as exclusive authority over a territory. This arrangement provided little incentive to sharply delineate territory. Military and political state limits rarely coincided, as state authority often extended beyond marked borders and into the neighboring territories. For example, Roman colonists often inhabited territories well beyond the imperial borders, and Roman armies often marched deep into barbarian lands for extended periods of time. The Egyptians and the Romans believed in the divine origins of their emperors and in the divine mission of their states. They saw the whole world as their empire, and thus they recognized no territorial limits (Pohl 2001). Reinforced imperial border lines were understood as temporary limits to be transcended in these empires' quest for universality.

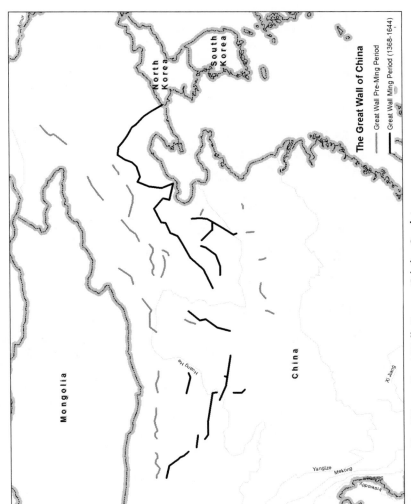

Figure 2.1 The Chinese Great Wall. *Source:* Cristina Scarlat.

For the early states, borders had a flexible meaning as outposts of their military power and authority. Early state limits were constituted by territories where authority faded away in transition to the surrounding areas. Despite the fact that borders occasionally assumed the appearance of sharp lines, a zonal rather than a linear understanding of borders was prevalent during antiquity (Whittaker 1994). State borders did not carry a political connotation similar to the one that current borders do, and they were not understood as the limits of a state's territorial power (Sahlins 1989). In this sense, they can be best understood as zonal frontiers rather than linear borders between sovereign states.

BORDERS DURING THE MEDIEVAL ERA

The medieval era was characterized by profound social and territorial fragmentation. The dominant features of state borders were temporal instability and territorial ambiguity. The relationship among territory, group identity, and state sovereignty differed significantly from that of antiquity. Its examination offers a unique perspective into the nature of borders in this period.

In medieval Europe, roughly between 500 and 1500, the territorial structure of political units, including duchies, principalities, kingdoms, empires, free cities, and others, was complex and overlapping. No particular territorial configuration of power dominated (J. Anderson 1996). Possession of territory was a highly contested matter. Territories changed hands frequently between ruling elites. A variety of political-territorial arrangements coexisted during this period. States were not imagined as contiguous, mutually exclusive territories (Ruggie 1993). It was common, for example, for one king to possess land inside the kingdom of another king. Moreover, when such arrangements were drafted, the extent of the territory of the enclave was rarely defined in terms of its borders but in terms of which villages and towns would belong to the new ruler. The control of cities and villages was more important than control of territory per se.

For most people, territorial identity was confined to the local village or town and did not extend to the entire royal territory. The nobility thought in terms of their territorial possessions, whose borders routinely changed through inheritance, marriage, or warfare (A. Murphy 1996). People from different parts of a kingdom did not typically relate to each other as inhabitants of the kingdom's territory but as subjects of the same ruler, or in terms of their ancestry. The ultimate allegiance of the population was to their rulers rather than to territorially defined, large-scale political communities. The only loyalty that transcended local group attachment was to the Christian Church (Heffernan 1998; Vincent 1987).

Political, military, religious, and other forms of medieval authority overlapped and interpenetrated (Brenner et al. 2003). It was possible for a king to have to pay taxes in his own kingdom while transiting the domain of a noble who was the king's subject. Authority was organized following functional rather than territorial logics. One could owe taxes in money to one ruler, in produce to the pope, and in military service to yet another ruler. Allegiance was owed to various rulers simultaneously, who could have been situated at different levels in the sociopolitical hierarchy—lords, dukes, bishops, and kings—as well as situated in different places. The ruler did not understand sovereignty over his or her domain in fixed territorial terms. In principle, one could "take office" anywhere, in any territory, as long as he or she came from the aristocracy (Ruggie 1993). Social status prevailed over ethnic origin and territorial descent.

The borders of the medieval state, inside as well as beyond Europe, were essentially fluid frontier zones. In Western and Central Europe during the Carolingian Empire in the eighth and ninth centuries, state frontiers acquired an individualized institutional form known as *marches*. Marches were organized frontier regions that ranged according to circumstances from districts well integrated within the state to newly acquired territories that were only partially organized and inhabited. Their general purpose was that of advanced defensive territories and transition zones, much in the same way as the Roman *limes* (Pohl 2001).

At the same time, records indicate that the concept of linear territorial borders was known and occasionally employed in various treaties during the medieval era. However, such fixed state borders did not have a concrete existence on the ground, and thus they were not meaningful realities in medieval society (Sahlins 1989). Despite the fact that occasionally state limits could have been marked by pillars or trenches, the medieval era was too turbulent, and social life was too precarious and localized to allow the implementation and the enforcement of territorially fixed state borders. What mattered most when at war, for example, was not the crossing of a state border line but whether any cities, villages, or nobility were captured. In this period, boundaries between class, property ownership, and religious affiliation were much more meaningful border lines than the territorial borders of the state.

Toward the end of the medieval period, during the thirteenth and fourteenth centuries, the nature of state borders began to change in Western Europe. Powerful kings in France and England, who resented sharing authority over their subjects with lower-rank nobles or with the church, managed to gain exclusive power over their territories. At this point, sovereignty was still understood in personalized terms, as authority over people rather than territory, but more precise state borders acquired increased importance in delimiting the extent of a king's absolute authority. It was during this period that political authority and exclusive territoriality started the slow process of convergence that eventually led to the replacement of porous frontiers with fixed border lines. Nonetheless, centuries passed before regions outside Western Europe experienced similar developments.

BORDERS DURING THE MODERN ERA

The origins of the modern state system and its privileging of territorial borders are often traced to the 1648 Peace of Westphalia that ended a period of ongoing war in Europe. The treaties drafted on this occasion established the concept of equality among states based on the principle of mutually exclusive sovereignty over territories delineated by borders (A. Murphy 1996; Taylor and Flint 2000). The politically centralized territorial state, free of outside interference, was seen as the appropriate solution for addressing the chronic lack of stability that characterized much of the medieval era. This reflected the changing nature of the state in Europe engendered by the ongoing territorialization of political and economical life. States became increasingly defined in territorial terms as individual spatial units where the impersonal authority of state institutions replaced the personal authority of the ruler. In this way, all other institutions or groups found inside a state's borders became subordinated to the state apparatus. People's identity started to change as well, as now authority could be exerted in different ways in different states. This meant that individuals could develop different life experiences according to the state they inhabited.

The most significant contribution of the Peace of Westphalia to the process of modern state border formation was the formalization of the principle of territorial sovereignty using territorial demarcation and control as its organizing logic (Albert 1998). Claiming absolute control over everything that falls inside state territorial limits set the spotlight on state borders. This claim had a twofold outcome for the nature of borders. First, it provided impetus for imagining territorially sharp border lines as state limits to avoid overlapping sovereignty claims. In political thinking and in international law, borders become sharp lines of territorial sovereignty that separated states and contained social relations inside a state's territory. The spatiality of state limits was reduced to a linear dimension. Second, it generalized the use of sharp territorial border lines, making it systemic. The geography of interstate limits changed from a network of diffuse and permeable frontiers to a grid of territorial borders (Giddens 1987; Paasi 1999).

This radical transformation in the organization of political space was influenced to a large extent by the advent of rationalist thinking in the seventeenth and eighteenth centuries that understood the world in terms of the supremacy of secular reason, deemed objective, over religious belief, which was increasingly deemed subjective. This perspective was accompanied by a transition from a relative understanding of space as multidimensional, fluid, and made up of a collection of places to an absolute understanding of space as unidimensional, stable, and uniform (Warf 2008). Sharp territorial state borders were in agreement with this new conceptualization of space.

The transition to the new state system did not take place overnight. Multiple allegiances continued to coexist for a long time before being displaced. It took centuries for the principle of state territorial sovereignty to replace old patterns of allegiance. Bordered state territorial sovereignty was a rather theoretical concept, as in practice sovereignty transgressions were the norm rather than the exception. However, the territorial sovereignty concept remained a powerful guiding principle of political-spatial organization, so powerful that it became difficult even to imagine other spatial systems of organizing power (Agnew 1994).

The early modern state borders only gradually assumed linear dimensions on the ground. During this period, linear borders coexisted with frontiers in some areas, while in other areas state limits switched back and forth between border lines and frontier zones (Sahlins 1989). Many European state borders were delimited now, although they were rarely demarcated. The absence of physical markers on the ground led to situations in which, despite the existence of a formal interstate border line, the de facto state limit continued to possess frontierlike characteristics. Generally, early modern territorial borders remained highly permeable for a wide range of exchanges.

During the eighteenth century, the concept of the territorial border as a political line of separation between states gained increased importance due to the emergence of nationalism and the institution of the nation-state (Sahlins 1989). Political-territorial borders as we know them today are only to be found following the emergence of the nation-state. In particular, the French Revolution in 1789 made a key contribution to the modern bundling of state, territorial sovereignty, group identity, and borders. Nationalism required an intimate connection between people and territory. This territorialization of identity materialized in the nation. The institution of the state gave the nation its political expression. Boundaries served to bind it all together. They helped maintain domestic coherence (the coherence of the nation) and regulate interactions with other nations.

The emergent form of state in Europe—the nation-state—represented a novel form of polity organized around a process of territorialization of social life. First, nationalism gave people a vital stake in the territorial state. Previously, the state mattered less for ordinary people as the state was not politically differentiated from the ruling class. The aristocracy *was* the state. Now the state claimed to include everybody living inside its borders. The state itself was nationalized. Second, people switched from being the subjects of a ruler to being citizens in a territory administered by a state apparatus that claimed to represent them directly. With the nation-state, people acquired a nationality based on their territorial residence. Third, the territory of the state became the territory of the nation as well. Now state territory was national territory. Fourth, sovereignty over state territory switched from the person of the ruler to the nation. That is, sovereignty became national sovereignty. Last but not least, the borders of the state became the borders of the nation as well. Now they were national borders, charged with holding together the social life inside the nation-state. In the same spirit, interstate borders became international borders, although there were rare occasions in which this term was actually correct since territorial borders routinely divided national groups.

Nevertheless, it was not until the nineteenth and the early twentieth centuries that the nation-state and its territorial borders become generalized. The idea that state and nation should territorially overlap underscored state formation processes in Europe after the Congress of Vienna in 1815 following the defeat of Napoleon. This idea culminated in 1919 at the Paris Peace Conference after the First World War, when the principle of national self-determination became the benchmark of the European political order (Taylor and Flint 2000). The nation-state became naturalized as the ultimate political expression of the will of a people and the uncontested modern political form of the organization of territory. The nationalization of state borders was now complete.

Nationalism proved difficult to apply in practice. Its original fallacy was to assume that people have common identities only because they happen to live inside the borders of a territory. Virtually all European states were composed of more than one national group. Thus the nation-state concept needed much help to take root. In order to generate the homogeneity that was necessary to build unitary nations to fit inside state borders, a host of practices were developed to instill a sense of a common national identity among the otherwise heterogeneous populations that inhabited the European states (B. Anderson 1991). In numerous cases, these practices have included the discursive production of Others on the neighboring side of the border. National borders have played a crucial role in the creation of myths and symbols to produce and enforce a clear division between the "superiority" of a nation's domestic "us" and the "inferiority" of its foreign "them" (Dalby 1998; Paasi 1996, 2003a). A sense of common national identity based on exclusion was achieved behind national borders. Through this process, national borders became sacrosanct to the nation-state. They became the guarantor of the very existence of the nation. Violating a state's borders represented an offense to the people themselves and a cause for war. Territorial aggression, either from another state or from inside the borders of a state, became aggression against the nation, not only against the state.

At the same time, the nationalization of state borders contributed to their naturalization. The notion of, and the need for, national borders became an unquestioned logic. Sharp, continuous border lines surrounding nation-states became a given, and national borders became the ubiquitous framework for thinking about the territorial organization of the world. It became very difficult to imagine social relations outside the spatial mold of the nation-state and its borders, or to challenge the purpose of national borders as regulators of social relations.

Many authors, such as Agnew (1998), Giddens (1987), Lefebvre (1991), Harvey (1989), Cox (2002), Wallerstein (1999), and others, call attention to the central role played by capitalism in the making of modern borders. They show how, despite the apparent contradiction between the barrier role of sharp national borders and the free flow of economic exchanges that capitalist relations of production require, capitalism and the nation-state borders had a symbiotic relationship in the sense that they reinforced each other by serving each other's needs. When compared to the territorial fragmentation of feudal markets and taxation systems, the unified territory of the nation-state provided an improved framework for the organization of stable large-scale wealth accumulation strategies. Sharp nation-state borders provided essential protection for national capital from outside competition, while at the same time they offered a readily available national market for consumption. Moreover, they have long played a central role in helping to raise revenue for the state from tax collection.

At the turn of the twentieth century, state borders could not be imagined as zonal frontiers anymore. Territorial border lines become standard bordering procedure for the organization of political space. Frontiers were reduced to lines even on the ground now, as interstate border demarcation, including fences and watchtowers, proceeded in earnest in Europe. Each round of national border consolidation gradually expanded the barrier function of state borders, deepening differences on both sides of the border. Borders accumulated a multitude of functions, from the political, to the cultural, to the economic, until they were imposed as borders between societies as well, succeeding in the end in circumscribing the whole spectrum of social life (Knippenberg and Markusse 1999; Taylor 1994).

Moreover, borders' importance went well beyond the status of territorial lines. They became institutionalized as part of the state apparatus. As state institutions of government in their own right, borders were

populated with specific infrastructural organization that included customs systems, border police officers, border guard military units, health
inspectors, and others.

However, it is essential to stress that despite the universality linear
borders have achieved both as bordering concepts and as bordering practices, state borders have retained in many instances frontierlike aspects
to this day (Sahlins 1989). In numerous cases, the physical presence of a
state linear border has not resulted in a thorough separation of the two
sides. Rather, social relations at the local scale often have continued to
stretch internationally recognized border lines, creating distinctive zonal
patterns of interaction that are in many ways similar to earlier frontiers. It
is more appropriate to think of borderlands rather than border lines when
attempting to critically understand modern interstate borders.

THE GLOBALIZATION OF BORDER LINES

So far we have seen that the making of modern interstate borders has
been an essentially European affair. Generally, states outside Europe
had political frontiers. This is not to say that linear borders did not exist
anywhere else in the world, or that non-Western societies would not have
imagined for themselves such state borders. Instead, linear nation-state
borders are a peculiar European creation that emerged out of Europe's
social, economic, and political historical circumstances to address European issues and to serve European worldviews. How is it, then, that this
single, context-specific model of political-territorial borders acquired contemporary global reach instead of, for example, several context-specific
border models coexisting in today's world? The answer can be found in
the process of European colonialism. With the exception of Japan, there
are no significant areas of the globe that have escaped the tutelage of one
European power or another during the six hundred years of European
colonialism. Even states that have maintained a formal status of independence such as China, Thailand, and Iran have been in effect fundamentally shaped by European colonial powers.

The two most notable exports of European colonialism have been
capitalism and the nation-state. Both of these have contributed to the globalization of modern state borders. The current linear political-territorial
borders outside Europe did not emerge from the local societies' imagination of how to divide political space. For the most part, these borders
were either imposed by Europeans or have been borrowed from them.
Non-Western societies had to adapt to these borders in the circumstances
of their integration into a world economic and political system dominated
by a few European powers. With independence in the nineteenth and

twentieth centuries, the new states usually retained the territorial borders they had as colonies. There were two main ways that colonial borders became contemporary interstate borders. First, the borders between different European colonial domains became interstate borders; for example, the border between the French Niger and the British Nigeria became the border between independent Niger and independent Nigeria. Second, the administrative borders between the subdivisions of a colonial domain became the new interstate borders; for example, the borders between the Spanish provinces in Latin America became the initial borders of the newly independent Latin American countries (Prescott 1965).

European colonialism began in the early 1400s with the Portuguese establishment of forts and trading posts along the west coast of Africa. By the end of the fifteenth century the Portuguese and the Spanish were competing in the colonization of South America. During the next century their rivalry expanded into Asia and the Pacific, thus reaching a global scale. During the seventeenth century several other European countries such as the Netherlands, France, and Britain joined the club of major colonial powers. Later, in the nineteenth century, Germany, Belgium, and Italy also acquired somewhat smaller overseas colonial domains.

The first notable colonial border dates from 1494, when Spain and Portugal decided how to divide their rights to colonize lands across the Atlantic they barely knew. In the Treaty of Tordesillas, the two colonial powers agreed to a north-south line along the 46 degrees, 37 minutes W meridian to separate their future colonial domains (Bruslé 2007; Elden 2005a) (see figure 2.2). As the geographical information about the new lands was scarce and incomplete only two years after Columbus stumbled upon them, the treaty provided that Spain and Portugal would later determine the exact location of the line and allocate lands accordingly. However, this never happened. When better maps became available, the Portuguese realized that their share of South America was much smaller than the Spanish one, and they pushed beyond the Tordesillas line. Eventually Brazil—the Portuguese colony in South America—occupied two-thirds of the continent.

The lasting significance of this famous dividing line consists in the principle it inaugurated. Establishing mathematically precise territorial border lines along meridians and parallels without regard for the patterns of social life in the divided lands became widespread colonial bordering practice. These were superimposed borders, dividing territories where no European had ever set foot. It was common that these borders were first established on paper in some European capital, and parties were later sent to find the actual location of the border on the ground. This produced numerous complications and disputes in the process of delineating colonial borders, often requiring later border adjustments (Foucher 1991; Prescott 1965).

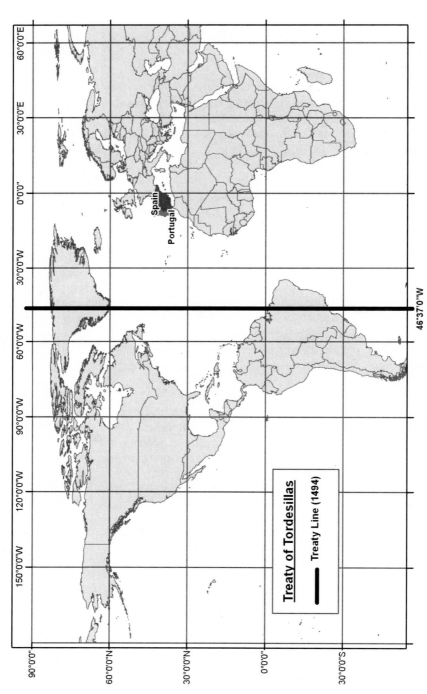

Figure 2.2 The Tordesillas Treaty line. *Source:* Cristina Scarlat.

Other common types of colonial borders included the so-called natural borders that followed mountain chains, shorelines, or river valleys, as well as buffer zones, protectorates, and neutral zones. The latter borders were intentionally conceived as zonal frontiers and could include large territories inhabited by one or several ethno-linguistic groups. They were primarily intended to prevent expanding European powers from fighting each other in the colonies, or to appease local populations that resisted direct European rule (Kratochwil 1986). Generally, the colonial borders appeared as distinct lines on the maps, but they were rarely demarcated and only if important resources were discovered nearby. In reality, they were rather permeable frontiers or borderlands (Bruslé 2007). For the most part they remained meaningless for the local populations who continued to cross them freely for a long time. Their main purpose was not to delineate European-style state territorial sovereignty but to delineate spheres of influence for the European powers. Colonial borders constituted effective ordering devices to help European powers organize a worldwide political-economic system that they controlled.

The 1894–1895 Berlin Conference, where the European powers gathered to establish their spheres of influence in Africa, typified colonial border making. Until the late nineteenth century, Africa had largely escaped extensive European colonization. However, by the 1880s, growing capitalist competition for resources among core European countries forced their attention to turn to Africa. In 1880 only about 10 percent of Africa was under European rule, and that was for the most part confined to the coasts. Only in the north and the south were there a few larger colonies that reached in the interior. Germany, Britain, France, Belgium, and Portugal entered a scramble for the resources of the continent by laying claims to various territories. The Berlin Conference was convened to set the rules for the colonization of Africa to avoid potentially conflicting claims (Prescott 1965). The outcome was the division of the continent, reorganizing about one thousand tribes into fifty states. Most of these states' borders were delineated by the colonizing powers in the first two decades following the conference. Geometric borders were generally used due to the lack of reliable information about the interior. By 1914, at the outset of World War I, virtually all of Africa was colonized with the exception of Liberia and Ethiopia (later to be occupied by Italy).

The independence of Latin American colonies from Spain and Portugal during the 1820s provides another opportunity for understanding the relationship between European colonialism and the globalization of linear state borders. The independence of Latin American countries, from Mexico in the north to Argentina and Chile in the south, represents an early instance of massive decolonization. This process provided the emerging states with unique opportunities to implement novel political-territorial forms of societal organization. Instead, the Latin American westernized elites borrowed the European ideology of nationalism and embarked upon the building of nation-states. This shows that decolonization started at a time when a worldwide political-economic system dominated by Europe was already in place. Indeed, chances for political-territorial and social innovation were genuine, but the weakness of the new political institutions encouraged few Latin American leaders to contemplate working outside the system.

The new states emerged along the administrative divisions of the Spanish colonial domain. Brazil remained united, keeping the borders it had had as a former Portuguese colony. The absence of significant Native Indian involvement in the region's independence movements provided little incentive to attempt to re-create preconquest political-territorial entities and borders or to devise new ones. The new elites, overwhelmingly Creole (American-born Spaniards), found that it was simply more efficient to use the inherited framework of colonial administrative borders than to start a new one. The problem was that these administrative boundaries were unclear and were sometimes ignored in the daily functioning of the colonial administrative apparatus (Prescott 1965). After independence, this state of affairs led to numerous border wars, disputes, and alterations. Formally, the political map of Latin America after the 1820s showed state borders as lines. For all practical purposes, they remained political frontiers for far longer. Geographical factors, such as dense tropical forests and the forbidding Andes Mountains, as well as lingering border disputes, made border demarcation difficult (Amilhat-Szary 2007). It was only at the end of the twentieth century that many of the disputed borders were demarcated.

KEY MOMENTS IN THE EMERGENCE
OF CONTEMPORARY STATE BORDERS

The idea of linear nation-state borders may have been globally diffused by the turn of the twentieth century, but border making was far from declining at this time. State borders kept emerging. The number of state borders at the beginning of the twentieth century was significantly lower than it was at the beginning of the twenty-first. This is not surprising if we consider that in the same period the number of independent states grew from 55 to 195, with 120 of them emerging after World War II (Paasi 2005). There are currently more than three hundred interstate land boundaries alone, and their number continues to grow with the emergence of new states. This shows that the world of borders exists in a state of flux: state borders constantly appear, disappear, or are altered.

During the twentieth century, three major border-making episodes can be identified that shaped the current world political map. The first took place in 1918 at the end of World War I and was concentrated in Europe. The disintegration of the Austro-Hungarian, German, Russian, and Ottoman empires resulted in an increase in the number of states in Central and Eastern Europe, as well as in territorial alterations to already existing ones. This led to a dramatic increase in the number of European state borders, from Yugoslavia and Czechoslovakia to Finland and the Baltic states.

At the same time, many Middle Eastern borders emerged on the world political map, although most of these would have to wait until after World War II to become interstate borders. Britain and France in particular played a crucial role in the making of Middle Eastern states and their borders. After occupying much of the Arab provinces of the defunct Ottoman Empire, they divided the territory between themselves and then started to carve up states and to draw borders. In effect, this amounted to a colonial partition of Arab lands. The borders of the newly created territorial entities such as Lebanon, Iraq, Kuwait, Jordan, and others included groups that displayed little desire for cohabitation (Blake 1992).

A second major moment of interstate border emergence took place after World War II and extended to the 1960s. This period is generally known as the decolonization era, and it coincides with the termination of the supremacy of European powers and the emergence of the bipolar Cold War world order. Decolonization led to the emergence of a majority of the world's interstate borders. It is also the most geographically expansive border-making period, as new states formed in the area stretching from the Middle East and Africa to Asia and the Pacific. The first new interstate borders to emerge were in the Middle East following the independence of Syria, Lebanon, and Jordan in 1946. This was followed by new interstate borders in Asia resulting from the independence of India in 1947; Burma in 1948; Indonesia in 1949; Vietnam, Cambodia, and Laos in 1954; Malaysia in 1957; and others. Lastly, a massive wave of new interstate borders appeared in Africa during the 1950s and 1960s when most of the African countries gained independence.

With a few exceptions, the new sovereign states retained superimposed colonial borders, thus inheriting the problems that these borders initially created. Moreover, a series of colonial-era developments aggravated existing border problems. For example, the widespread colonial practice of charging ethnic or religious minority groups with running the administrative affairs of the colonies pitted local ethnic and religious groups against each other and resulted in numerous postindependence secessionist demands, civil wars, and interstate conflicts. At the same time, the spatial economic and political polarization of numerous colonies between the better-off coastal regions and the peripheral interior regions created resentment among various populations and also led to considerable upheaval. While these issues generated significant pressure for border change, it is remarkable how little border change actually took place during the postindependence era. The primary rationale for preserving the grid of colonial borders was concern for the stability of the world system (Herbst 1989). The new leaders, as well as the leaders of the two Cold War superpowers, believed that the modification of colonial borders would lead to global chaos given the seemingly intractable issues that colonial borders raised. Instead, the maintenance of these borders led to more localized and manageable chaos. The United States and the USSR did wage proxy wars by arming opposing factions throughout the postcolonial world, but they were rarely supportive of extensive interstate border changes that they perceived to have the potential to destabilize the entire world system.

The third round of contemporary interstate border expansion came during the 1990s in the aftermath of the Cold War. Several multiethnic states disintegrated and were succeeded by new ones, while a few divided states united. Geographically, the majority of the new borders emerged in Europe, but Eastern Africa, the Middle East, and Central Asia also experienced border changes. Czechoslovakia gave way to the Czech and Slovak republics. Yugoslavia descended into civil war and spawned seven separate states. The USSR dissolved and was replaced by fifteen new states, five of which lie in Central Asia. Eritrea seceded from Ethiopia. West and East Germany, as well as North and South Yemen, united. In numerous instances the borders of these new states were contested both from inside and outside, and subsequent wars ensued, leading to even more contested borders, such as in the Caucasus region, Moldova, and elsewhere.

These developments resulted in a dramatic increase in the number of interstate borders. Tens of thousands of miles of new borders emerged on the world political map during the 1990s (Foucher 2007). The territorial convulsions of this era continue to be felt today, as demonstrated by the independence of Kosovo in 2008, as well as the 2008 war in the Caucasus between Russia and Georgia over the separatist enclaves of South Ossetia and Abkhazia.

These major border-making episodes of the twentieth century attest to the monopoly that modern state borders hold over geographical imaginations of social and political life. Societies continue to be conceptualized as contained by territorially linear state borders, and political independence cannot be imagined without state border lines. Following a circular logic, despite old borders being dismantled at one time because they are considered constrictive by one group or another, this is done only to reerect new borders, with the belief that this time around the borders will be the "right" ones and will endure forever. The new borders usually only last until other groups, at another time, decide that they can do even better. What is absent here is the will to search for answers beyond borders and bordering, and perhaps to transcend borders and bordering altogether.

3

Borders in the
Era of Globalization

BORDER LINES MEET GLOBAL FLOWS

During the closing decades of the twentieth century, globalization-related developments have challenged the exclusive bundling of sovereignty, territory, identity, and borders claimed by nation-states. Increasingly, the territorial scope of economic, political, social, and cultural processes does not overlap the borders of the state. These processes are developing their own sets of borders that transcend the borders of the state. In other words, these processes are each bounded in different ways (Christiansen and Jorgenson 2000). At stake is the paramount role territorial borders play in the organization of space. The normative view of state borders as containers of social relations and regulators of interstate interaction does not account for the proliferation of global flows of capital, people, goods, and ideas (J. Anderson and O'Dowd 1999; M. Anderson and Bort 2001). These flows are transnational, nonstate phenomena that relate to space in different ways than state institutions do. They follow logics of spatial organization that diverge from the logic of the territorial container that state border lines represent. Border making works in different ways for flows than it works for fixed state territories.

The tension between state border lines and flows of exchange is not a new phenomenon. During the modern era there has always been a measure of cross-border investment, trade, and migration that raised challenges to the capacity of borders to fully contain social relations inside state territories. The need for coordination among states to achieve certain shared goals, such as participation in international organizations, regional alliances, and large-scale infrastructure projects, is in large part responsible for maintaining a certain degree of permeability for most state borders. As a result, border permeability has functioned as a regulatory mechanism for interstate exchange flows.

However, the nature of current globalization flows is generating notable departures from this traditional relationship. Past cross-border exchanges were generally intermittent, geographically specific, and selective in their nature. They did not take place twenty-four hours a day, they occurred only in certain areas, and they covered a rather limited range of products and activities. Consequently, border permeability was not a generalized condition. Twenty-first-century global flows differ in several key ways. First, the speed with which they move through space has increased dramatically with the help of new telecommunication technologies such as the Internet and optic fiber and with the improvement of air, land, and water transportation networks. Second, their duration has changed as they have become constant. Third, their number and diversity have multiplied greatly, thus becoming a generalized condition in numerous societies. Fourth, their geography has shifted from primarily interstate to primarily supra-, sub-, multi- and transstate scales. Global flows tend to pass *through*, rather than simply run *between*, state territories. This is the condition that the term "global flows" attempts to capture. The institution of the state itself has been decentered as the primary locus of origin and destination of these contemporary flows (Sassen 2006). This does not mean that flows have lost their territorial grounding and that state territory has become irrelevant to them. Instead, it means that states do not exclusively organize, and their territorial borders do not exclusively regulate, flows of exchange. Global flows have replaced interstate flows as the primary framework for organizing exchanges in space.

Issues that exemplify contemporary challenges to the power of state borders to regulate social relations in space permeate numerous spheres of society, from economics, to politics, to culture. Their outcomes are wide ranging, and they have the power to produce systemic change. The following sections illustrate a series of key instances in which global flows meet border lines, and the terms of these encounters are discussed.

THE STRUCTURE OF THE INTERNATIONAL ECONOMY

Economic processes that span the globe constitute the leading contemporary challenges transcending modern state borders. At the heart of the matter are profound structural changes taking place in capitalism. Capitalism is undergoing a multifaceted restructuring of its relationship with space that includes the readjustment of its symbiotic ties with the nation-state. With time, the mutually exclusive territorial logic of the nation-state system became constrictive for the internal logics of capitalist organization of production and exchange (Harvey 2000). To the extent that capitalism continually strengthened its position during the twentieth century as the world's dominant economic and ideological system, state borders became less important as mechanisms for protecting domestic markets from outside competition.

After the 1970s, neoliberal ideas of free-market economics and market-based development welcomed worldwide competition as a new strategy of wealth accumulation at a global scale and denounced national protectionism as an outdated development strategy. "Free trade," capitalism's mantra for almost two hundred years, became globalization's unofficial doctrine. State borders came to be seen primarily in terms of *costs* of exchange and *barriers* to trade that have to be overcome to allow unimpeded trade flows essential to the existence of free markets. Thus, perceptions of borders shifted from "solutions" to "problems" for capital accumulation. This is how the "open borders" discourse achieved prominence during the 1990s to become the most important factor shaping the creation of a new global border regime.

Financial Services

International financial markets exemplify the spatial logic of economic activity at a global scale. Financial services, including banking, insurance, securities, and others, have long been the leading sector of economic globalization. They have played a central role in opening up state borders to global trade flows. Much of the international financial system is concentrated in a few strategically located trading centers linked in a global network by digital telecommunication superhighways (Sassen 2001). The digital nature of global funds has turned them into extremely liquid money. Massive, multi-trillion-dollar electronic financial flows circle the globe with the speed of light every day with little regard to state borders. The twenty-four-hour trading day starts in Tokyo, when it is evening in New York; then trading moves to London, then to New York, where it lasts until the market is ready to open again in Tokyo (Warf 1989). A series of intermediary financial centers from Hong Kong to Singapore to Abu Dhabi to Paris to Los Angeles cover eventual time lags in the trading day among financial centers. The total daily volume of electronic financial transactions is staggering. In 2010, the average daily global trade in foreign currency alone reached $4 trillion, while the average daily global trade in goods and services amounted to only approximately $30 billion (Bank for International Settlements 2010). This means that one day of currency trades on the world's financial markets accounts for over 20 percent of the trade in goods and services in an entire year.

The spatial logic of global financial flows has deep implications for the regulatory power of state territorial borders. The dazzling speed and volatility of electronic money flows profoundly affect national money supplies and inflation, interest, and exchange rates, as well as taxation revenues, financial criminality, and other issues that have long been considered components of state sovereignty. Traditionally, state borders have defined the territorial scope of these issues. In the twenty-first century, they operate on a global scale, outside the exclusive control of state governments. Massive amounts of money can be invested in a national market at a moment's notice when investors perceive favorable conditions for capital accumulation (Warf 2002). At the same time, investors can rapidly withdraw money from a national market if they perceive political instability or unfavorable economic policies. In this case, the consequences can be devastating for the local economy. National governments have relatively little control over the flow of money in and out of their economies, as demonstrated by the financial meltdowns of the 1990s in Southeast Asia, Russia, and Mexico, and by the 2008 worldwide recession that started in the United States and rapidly engulfed the entire global economy.

Manufacturing

Transnational corporations (TNCs) constitute another edifying example of the tension between state borders and global flows. They are often capital-intensive companies operating in more than one country, frequently through subsidiaries and subcontractors integrated in a global production network. During the last two decades, their number and scope have vastly increased, driven by the desire to profit from comparative advantages such as cheaper labor, lower taxes, and consumer markets, among others, that different national markets offer. In 2007 there were an estimated 79,000 TNCs employing over one hundred million people worldwide, and 790,000 foreign affiliates (United Nations Conference on Trade and Development 2008). TNCs generate over two-thirds of the world trade and foreign direct investment, effectively displacing states as the main agents of international trade. The largest TNCs, such as Walmart, ExxonMobil, General Electric, Toyota, and others have annual revenues larger than the GDP of many countries. Thus TNC investment decisions have the power to affect a country's economy and politics. In order to make their markets attractive for TNC activities, governments often pursue economic policies that are determined by rationales originating from outside their borders.

Twenty-first-century TNCs do not organize their activities with the territory of their home nation-state in mind. Rather, the essence of their spatial logic is to think about their activities with the global space in mind. State borders remain important in this process because they induce regional differences that TNCs seek to take advantage of. However, TNC activities are not limited by these borders. TNCs' core rationale is to function above these borders, at a larger spatial scale. Low transport costs and free-trade agreements allow them to easily transcend state borders.

Generally, TNC activities reach inside state borders to exploit whatever local resources may be available there; then they transfer these resources to another country or region to process them, and then trade the final product on the global market. For example, major auto TNCs maintain their administrative headquarters in developed-world countries, while their assembly factories are spread throughout the world. Their final product can include a major percentage of parts and subassemblies produced in numerous places around the world. Thus a Volkswagen bought in the United States, for example, can hardly be called a German-made car as it may include a majority of its parts made in other locations than Germany, and it may be assembled in Mexico. To make this global spatial logic of production work, highly permeable state borders are essential.

The same global-market logic was at work in one of the first major twenty-first-century public health scares involving the United States, China, and several other countries. In 2007, a series of unexpected pet deaths led to the discovery of massive amounts of melamine-contaminated pet food supplies sold in U.S. supermarkets. Soon melamine contamination was discovered in human food supplies as well, from chicken to fish to infant milk formula (Fuller et al. 2008). Then the debacle expanded to include toxic toys coated with lead-based paint. Massive, multi-billion-dollar food and toys recalls followed in the United States and elsewhere. The geography of this scandal pointed unequivocally toward China since the contaminated products originated somewhere inside its borders. Thus the blame fell squarely on China. Melamine, when added to certain food products, can artificially increase their protein level and make the product cheaper. Also, lead-based paint is cheaper than its alternatives. It appears that several Chinese manufacturers attempted to cut corners and used these illegal substances in order to decrease the costs of their supplies.

However, a critical interrogation of this geography reveals that the borders between China and the United States were so blurred that it is irrelevant to assign blame to any single country. This was not a classic trade situation where products made by firms in one country were imported in another and then sold in the latter's domestic market. The contaminated products did not display Chinese brand names. Instead they were sold in the global market under some of the largest and most well-established brand names in the United States, like Tyson Foods, Mattel, Fisher-Price, and numerous others. When buying these products, consumers did not pay Chinese companies but were paying U.S. companies and expected the U.S. standards of quality that these companies boast. The problem was created by the global production model that food and toy TNCs follow today. They use production facilities in countries such as China that offer cheap labor and other incentives to drive down the price. These sites can be either directly owned by a TNC, or local subcontractors can be used to supply various parts of the product. In either case the final product is made in China but bears the label of the owning TNC. The bulk of the profits resulting from the sale of the product go to the TNC that owns the label. While it is true that the contamination happened in China, the responsibility lies with the TNCs that sold the product under their name. Following the logic of nation-state borders, both Chinese and U.S. borders were equally responsible for not preventing the contamination by failing to detect and intercept the contaminated products at border-crossing checkpoints. Nonetheless, following the logic of the global market, no state border could have stopped the contaminated products since the TNCs' spatial logic purposefully transcends state borders. Ultimately, the responsibility rests with the TNCs themselves, which are expected to take on the regulatory functions that state borders previously performed.

Global Economic Institutions

International institutions such as the International Monetary Fund (IMF), the World Bank, and the World Trade Organization (WTO), to name only the most well known, are central to the structure of the global economy (Sassen 2006). The IMF and the World Bank are institutions that predate the globalization era. They function much like international investment and development banks, lending money to national governments in need, usually in the developing world. Their membership rules, which require governments to pay a quota proportional to the size of their economy, give developed countries overwhelming power to influence lending policies and strategies.

During the 1980s these institutions adopted neoliberal "free-market" policies as their guiding principle. Countries that wish to borrow money are required to implement a set of austerity measures designed to structurally readjust their economies to "free-market" norms. Reducing inflation, devaluing currencies, cutting government spending on social projects and subsidies to the poor, and privatization of key public services are policies primarily intended to meet the investment needs of TNCs and finance capital headquartered inside the borders of developed countries.

In turn, implementing these changes ostensibly allows the borrowing countries to save enough money to repay their debts. Nonetheless, such policies are not designed to alleviate the effects of the crises these countries face. Cutting government spending at a time of soaring unemployment, when the government should increase spending to help weather the economic crisis, comes at great cost to the local societies and fuels widespread popular resentment.

The fact that in the last two decades the vast majority of developing countries have taken IMF or World Bank loans demonstrates the power of these institutions to reshape the international economy according to "free-market" and "open borders" principles. Recently, even developed countries such as Iceland and Britain have asked for IMF loans. In more extreme cases, the IMF has temporarily run the financial affairs of countries in crisis, as has happened in Bulgaria in 1997 and Argentina in 2002. When governments implement economic policies designed outside their borders and that are outside of their control, they implicitly endorse the unraveling of the relationship between territorial borders and state sovereignty as it was constructed during the early modern era.

The WTO was established in 1995 to provide a multinational framework for regulating global trade. Its mission is to promote "free trade" by eliminating barriers to trade such as national tariffs, subsidies, import quotas, and other protectionist measures. The WTO includes almost all states of the world, which combined account for over 97 percent of world trade. The institution can settle trade disputes and make trade rules, and it has the power to enforce trade sanctions against noncompliant members. This also means that the adoption of WTO agreements by national governments contributes to the diminishing power of territorial borders to control trade flows.

THE ENVIRONMENT

Environmental issues have always transcended state borders. Drought or flooding has never stopped at a state's borders. Air, water, and soil pollution, such as acid rain, toxic spills, and poisonous waste, care little for territorial borders. The idea that socially constructed border lines can contain the impact of human activity on the natural environment appears absurd. Yet modern state territorial sovereignty suggests just this—a state is free to use the natural environment inside its borders in whatever way it pleases. This conceptualization of environmental issues at a particular spatial scale limits our understanding of these issues as well as our ability to identify sustainable solutions for them (O'Lear 2010). At the beginning of the twenty-first century there are few if any truly global environmental standards that are legally binding (Angel et al. 2007). The grid of state border lines continues to provide the primary spatial framework for addressing complex global environmental issues.

Globalization has transformed the relationship between the environment and territorial border lines in at least two fundamental ways. First, it has exacerbated the consequences of existing environmental issues and has created new ones. These developments made border lines appear even more redundant when it comes to the environment. Second, globalization has increased global awareness of acute environmental issues, which in turn has generated transnational solidarity and demands for global action. Global climate change and the Kyoto Protocol are good illustrations of these two situations.

Global Climate Change

During the first decade of the twenty-first century, anthropogenic global climate change has emerged as the most severe contemporary environmental issue and has succeeded in attracting worldwide attention. The steady increase in the average temperature of the earth's atmosphere over the last several decades has been generated in large part by human-made emissions such as carbon dioxide, methane, and other gases released through fossil fuel combustion and deforestation. The accumulation of these gases in the atmosphere has enhanced the greenhouse effect that is causing a rapid overheating of the earth's surface.

Historically, most anthropogenic greenhouse gas emissions originated from inside the borders of a relatively small number of developed countries. Since the nineteenth century, the burning of fossil fuels that release carbon dioxide has powered the industrialization process. Until recently, the United States has been the largest producer of carbon dioxide emissions. With globalization, developing countries like China and India have also emerged as major contributors to greenhouse gas emissions, thus worsening an already critical situation. In 2006, China has replaced the United States as the world's largest producer of carbon dioxide emissions. However, in terms of per capita emissions, the United States remains the largest contributor.

Deforestation is the second major contributor to greenhouse gas emissions. First, the use of fire to clear up forests releases carbon dioxide into the atmosphere. Second, the shrinking of the forest coverage deprives the earth of a highly effective carbon dioxide reservoir, as trees naturally store carbon dioxide from the atmosphere. Rampant deforestation in the tropical forests of Amazonia and Borneo is technically a Brazilian or Indonesian domestic problem, respectively. However, deforestation inside these countries' borders exacerbates the greenhouse effect that impacts the entire globe. To make things more complex, deforestation in these places is not primarily driven by domestic consumption needs. The rising demand for lumber, beef, soybeans, and palm oil in developed countries significantly contributes to the replacement of forests by large-scale plantations and farms in developing countries.

Worldwide acknowledgment that the harmful potential presented by global climate change can be tackled only by transnational action has led to the adoption of the 1997 Kyoto Protocol under the UN framework. Although state borders still provide the spatial framework for policy implementation, this is the first international environmental treaty to provide a global road map for the reduction of greenhouse gas emissions. It includes legally binding commitments for member states to cut emissions to reach preset targets (Kyoto Protocol 1998). However, the effectiveness of the Kyoto Protocol has been crippled by the refusal of the United States to sign the treaty.

Global climate change is already having other direct impacts on state borders. Rising ocean levels are submerging low-lying islands from the Indian to the Pacific oceans, creating the prospect of mass migrations of environmental refugees from these islands to developed states like Australia, New Zealand, and beyond (K. Marks 2006). In the Arctic, the melting of the polar ice cap has opened up the ocean to more reliable navigation lines and to the exploitation of mineral resources. This situation has sparked an intense race between nearby states like Russia, Canada, Norway, and others to expand their sovereignty over Arctic waters by formally determining their external borders on the continental shelf (Reynolds 2007). This point was made very clear in 2007 when a Russian submarine symbolically planted a Russian flag on the seabed right under the North Pole (Dodds 2008; Steinberg 2010).

Pandemics

Pandemics are another example illustrating twenty-first-century dynamics between environmental factors and territorial borders. Viral outbreaks such as SARS, the avian flu, and the swine flu have recently spread from continent to continent like wildfire. The speed and frequency of global travel and trade make such diseases difficult to contain by state borders. For example, the 2003 SARS pandemic spread within days from East Asia to North America and Europe through air travel (Ali and Keil 2006). Similarly, the 2009 swine flu pandemic rapidly diffused from North America to the rest of the world.

Another example is the avian flu. This is a virus that occurs naturally in birds and is generally harmless to them. In 2004 the virus started to become more contagious and passed to domesticated birds such as chickens and ducks, which then passed it to humans. The virus started traveling from Vietnam and Thailand to China, and then to Russia; in 2006 it arrived in Africa and Eastern Europe, and it reached the British Isles later that year. The virus appeared unstoppable, and for good reason. The disseminating agents were migratory birds that knew no territorial borders. While avian flu–related human casualties have been very limited so far, the virus wreaked havoc on domestic birds, especially chickens. Hundreds of millions had to be culled in a worldwide effort to contain the virus.

These viral outbreaks have exposed the limited efficacy state borders provide to tackle such circumstances (Fidler 2003). The most common responses from state governments have consisted of imposing travel bans to the affected areas, reinforcing border controls, and quarantining people suspected of being affected by the viruses. At the same time, these outbreaks have revealed the need for transnational institutions capable of effectively tackling pandemics, such as the UN's World Health Organization, which provided much-needed, timely, global-level coordination in the fight against SARS, the avian flu, and the swine flu.

HUMAN RIGHTS

Human rights are representative of challenges to state borders in the legal realm. The UN's Universal Declaration of Human Rights of 1948 marked the beginning of the contemporary human rights regime. Its goal was to establish a set of universal norms for governing the treatment of people by their states in order to help prevent a repeat of the horrors of World War II. In the intervening period, an international human rights regime has been gradually developed through a series of international treaties and institutions that have transformed human rights standards into legally binding and enforceable state obligations. Components of this regime are located at many scales, ranging from the International Criminal Court (ICC) and the UN Human Rights Council at the supranational level, to regional bodies such as the European Court of Human Rights, to national human rights laws that claim universal or extraterritorial jurisdiction, to transnational nongovernmental organizations (NGOs) such as Amnesty International.

External Interventions

The international human rights regime is often at odds with state borders. The problem resides in the enforceability of human rights by the international community, which can be interpreted as a loss of sovereignty (Camilleri 2004). Traditionally, human rights have fallen under national jurisdiction whose spatial extent was delineated by state borders. When states ratify legally binding international human rights treaties, they are obliged to incorporate these norms into national law. At the same time, ratification also opens up the possibility of external enforcement by other parties to the treaty in case of noncompliance. Until recently, external interference has been a rare occurrence, as national governments have generally been the ultimate instance of enforcement. However, this situation changed significantly during the 1990s with the emergence of several international human rights courts endowed with jurisdiction to prosecute human rights abuses committed inside the borders of a state. The International Criminal Tribunals for the former Yugoslavia in 1993 and for Rwanda in 1994 are among the best known examples to date.

Arguably the most important outcome of the international human rights regime over the last half century is the broad recognition that human rights have achieved at the individual as well as the state level (Camilleri 2004). Despite the fact that nonintervention is the central principle governing international relations, during the last two decades external interference inside the borders of a state has become more acceptable on humanitarian grounds if there is proof of massive and systematic human rights violations (S. Murphy 1996). At the same time, the fact that many of these interventions further aggravated human rights violations points to the risk that "humanitarian reasons" can be used by more powerful states as a facade for interventionist or neoimperialist policies (Elden 2005b; Falah et al. 2006). The currency of humanitarian intervention inside state borders, with or without UN mandate, is exemplified by the numerous interventions in the conflicts in Liberia (1990), northern Iraq (1990), Somalia (1992), Rwanda (1994), Haiti (1994 and 2004), Bosnia (1995), Sierra Leone (1998 and 2000), Kosovo (1999), East Timor (1999 and 2006), Ivory Coast (2004 and 2011), and Libya (2011). Even the case for the U.S. involvement in Afghanistan (2001) and Iraq (2003) was in part made on humanitarian grounds.

The principle of universal jurisdiction is a new and highly controversial outcome resulting from the incorporation of human rights norms into national law. It can allow national courts jurisdiction over genocide and other crimes against humanity committed by anybody, anywhere in the world. Universal jurisdiction takes the conflict between the international human rights regime and bordered state sovereignty to a new level. The landmark case occurred in 1998 when a Spanish judge indicted the former Chilean dictator Augusto Pinochet for crimes against humanity committed in his own country during his years in power (Byers 2000). Pinochet was seeking medical treatment in London at the time of his indictment, and the British government arrested him in order for him to be extradited to Spain. In a compromise decision, the British government released him in 2000 to freely return to Chile, where he was indicted again, this time by Chilean judges. Eventually Pinochet died in 2006 without being convicted of any crimes. Similar cases prosecuted in Spanish courts during the last decade include former Peruvian president Alberto Fujimori and several Argentine officers involved in the juntas of the 1970s.

In a recent development, the high casualty toll among Palestinian civilians during the 2008–2009 Gaza war between Israel and Hamas has raised questions of human rights violations by the Israeli military. Although no official indictment has been issued against Israeli military personnel, the Israeli government has expressed concerns that its soldiers can be prosecuted while traveling abroad by European courts claiming universal jurisdiction (McGirk 2009). The fact that powerful governments like Israel are taking seriously the possibility of external jurisdiction over alleged human rights crimes indicates the significant challenges the international human rights regime raises to state borders.

The International Criminal Court

The latest and most ambitious addition to the human rights regime is the International Criminal Court, established in 2002 and sanctioned by a majority of world states. The ICC is the first permanent international tribunal and represents the first ever attempt to implement justice on a global scale. The court has jurisdiction over the most severe human rights abuses such as genocide, war crimes, and crimes against humanity committed anywhere inside the borders of its member states or by a citizen of its member states (Rome Statute of the ICC 1998). In addition, its jurisdiction can extend to nonmember states if the UN Security Council asks the ICC to open investigations. However, the ICC is designed to complement national laws, not replace them. It can exercise jurisdiction only when national courts are unwilling or unable to prosecute such crimes. In addition, other human rights abuses continue to remain the purview of national law.

Several powerful states, most prominently the United States, India, and China, have refused so far to recognize or join the ICC, fearing loss of sovereignty and the possibility of politically motivated prosecutions of their citizens. U.S. reservations toward the court are representative of the nature of the encounter between globalization and territorial borders. The United States has for a long time been one of the most ardent supporters of international human rights and has praised itself for a domestic justice system that vigorously protects human rights. In appearance, there is little reason for the United States to have reservations about the ICC, as their goals with regard to human rights are similar. However, the superpower status of the United States has led to its involvement in numerous crisis situations around the world. Thus the potential that its citizens could be accused of human rights violations is significant. What U.S. leaders fear is the possibility of trading the familiarity of justice inside their national borders with the much less familiar, yet seen by many around the world as more legitimate, global justice.

The first trial at the ICC began in 2009 and deals with war crimes committed by militia leaders in Congo during 2002–2003. In addition, the court has received complaints of human rights violations in numerous countries, has opened several investigations into various conflicts, and has issued arrest warrants for several people (ICC Outreach Report 2008). In 2009, the ICC indicted the Sudanese president Omar al-Bashir for crimes against humanity and war crimes committed in Darfur. This event constitutes the latest human rights regime milestone. It is the first time a sitting president has been indicted by the ICC for human rights violations in an ongoing conflict in his own country. The outcomes of such global justice still remain to be seen.

TRANSNATIONAL TERRORISM

Transnational terrorism is primarily defined as politically or ideologically motivated violence that involves the crossing of an interstate border. From a geographical perspective, transnational terrorist organizations display a networked structure that enables them to move through borders from state to state with relative impunity. These networks have noticeable mobility-related advantages when compared with the rigidity of territorial state borders. Under these circumstances, traditional enforcement of state borders has limited effects on the overall movement inside the terrorist networks that span them.

Transnational terrorism can have multiple causes and can include state as well as nonstate actors. While state-supported terrorism has decreased considerably after the end of the Cold War, nonstate-sponsored terrorism has significantly increased. The most spectacular terror acts starting with the 1990s have been perpetrated by self-supporting organizations that work across state borders. Their motivations are grounded in large part in religious fundamentalist ideology and are different from earlier terrorist organizations that relied mainly on political ideology or separatism. Their political goals are also more global in scope and more vaguely defined, in contrast with the more localized aims and specific political demands of earlier terrorist networks.

Islamic Fundamentalist Terrorist Networks

At the beginning of the twenty-first century, Islamic fundamentalist terrorism has become the face of transnational terrorism, effectively eclipsing other types of terrorist networks grounded in ethnic separatism, political ideology, or fundamentalist ideology inspired by other religions. Al-Qaeda is the transnational terrorist organization that has become the archetype of Islamic fundamentalist terrorism, embodying its defining characteristics. Al-Qaeda is commonly described as a "network of networks" formed by loosely associated groups, dispersed, decentralized, and without a clear hierarchy of command. It uses tools like the World Wide Web, mobile telephones, satellite telecommunications, electronic banking, and jetliners to coordinate its actions, to enable movement through state borders without detection, and to disseminate its ideology (Watts 2007). Al-Qaeda threats appear to be borderless, present everywhere at once.

However, this view is misleading due to the fact that the ubiquitous state territoriality model has largely obscured the understanding of other forms of territoriality. Al-Qaeda is not just a blend of transborder deterritorialized networks (Elden 2007a). While these networks do not claim sovereignty over the territory of any particular state and have no linear borders to defend, they do need places to work as network hubs to provide operational bases and staging grounds for terror attacks. A worldwide array of Muslim quasi-states, from Somalia and Sudan to Afghanistan and Pakistan, offers locations for territorial bases without the responsibilities of territorial sovereignty. At the same time, transnational terrorist hubs are not limited to states with tenuous sovereignty inside their borders, as demonstrated by the existence of terrorist cells in Florida, Hamburg, Madrid, and London.

State Reactions to Transnational Terrorism

The U.S. response to al-Qaeda attacks both before and after September 11, 2001, underlines the limitations of state borders in addressing global terrorism. In a world full of border lines, only comprehensive cross-border collaboration can offer an effective avenue for counteracting transnational terror networks. The problem is that the complex level of institutional cooperation this undertaking requires is virtually impossible to achieve in practice since there is no adequate global infrastructure to allow institutions in various countries to share vital information in a way that transcends the taboos of state sovereignty. Instead of working to build the necessary transnational infrastructure to overcome the segmented nature of government-to-government information sharing, the U.S. response to al-Qaeda has been marked by an inability to think outside the framework of state borders. Not accidentally, the first action taken after September 11, 2001, has been the closing of the U.S. borders, implying that these territorial lines could restore the violated sense of security many people felt. The fact that these borders were not effective in stopping the perpetrators' network in the first place was lost on many American policy makers.

The major U.S. initiative for addressing transnational terrorism has consisted in launching a "Global War on Terror" whose primary objective has been to identify states where al-Qaeda hubs are located in order to take military action against them. While the term *global* might have suggested a constructive multilateral effort to involve the global community in combating terrorism, the word *war* was reminiscent of the antagonistic power politics practices in which the powerful impose on the weak. The U.S. War on Terror has indeed reached a global scale, with U.S. troops and intelligence operations deployed worldwide. Nonetheless, this effort has been highly unilateral, falling short of building a concerted global effort to tackle the roots of transnational terrorism. The logic of this war assumed that nonstate transnational Islamic fundamentalist terrorism can be defeated by classical military might deployed against territorial states. This strategy conflated the presence of terrorist bases inside the borders of a state with the commitment of that state to supporting terrorism, overlooking the fact that in some instances central governments may not be in a position to fight the terrorists because they may not control the entire territory of the state (Elden 2007a).

Afghanistan, where a clear connection between the Islamic fundamentalist Taliban regime and al-Qaeda can be documented, was an early theater in the Global War on Terror. The ousting of the Taliban from power in 2001 rid the Afghan population of a tyrannical regime but has done little to tackle Islamic fundamentalist terrorist networks. In the ten years that have followed, al-Qaeda has franchised Islamic terrorism worldwide and together with the Taliban has regrouped in neighboring Pakistan under the shelter of interstate borders. From there they have played a deadly cat-and-mouse game with U.S. troops in Afghanistan, who cannot pursue them across the border into Pakistan given that this is an allied state according to the state-by-state approach to terrorism. To compensate for the lack of military presence inside the borders of Pakistan, the U.S. military has embarked on a regular air bombing campaign of that country's northwest tribal borderlands hosting al-Qaeda and Taliban strongholds. These operations, which often come with severe costs in civilian life, are justified in military terms in order to counteract the border-transcending logic of terrorist networks. Nonetheless, the very act of a state's army bombing the territory of another sovereign state that is not at war represents a flagrant violation of the sovereignty principle. The fact that this appears to be done with the acquiescence of the Pakistani government stresses even more the quandary the bundling of territorial borders and state sovereignty faces today.

The unorthodox nature of the Global War on Terror, involving a state with fixed borders that is bound by international law to follow certain

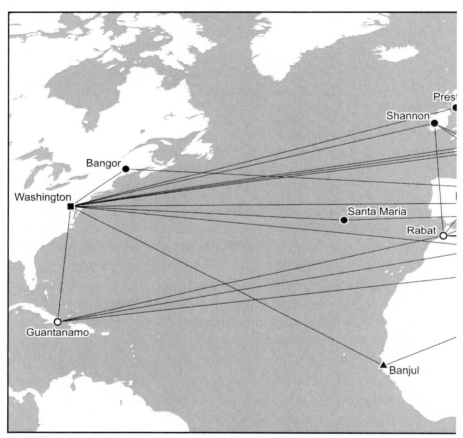

Figure 3.1 The global infrastructure of secret CIA detention sites and interstate transfers. Reprinted from J. D. Sidaway, "Intervention: The Dissemination of Banal Geopolitics: Webs of Extremism and Insecurity," *Antipode* 40, no. 1 (2008): 2–8, with permission from John Wiley & Sons

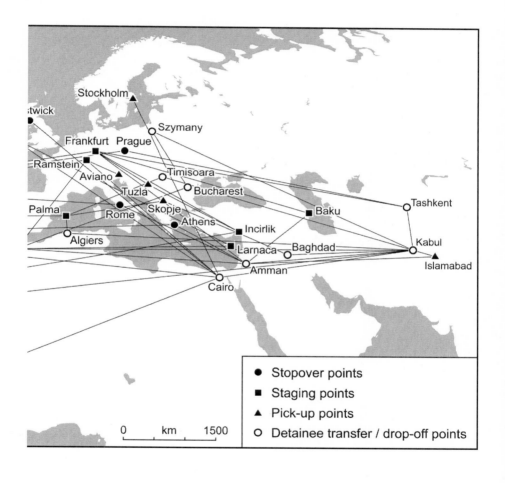

Stockholm ▲

○ Szymany

Frankfurt ■ Prague ●

■ Ramstein

Aviano ▲

Tuzla ▲ ○ Bucharest

Rome ● Skopje ▲

Palma ■ Athens ●

○ Algiers

stwick ●

○ Timisoara

Baku ■

○ Tashkent

■ Incirlik

Larnaca ■ ○ Baghdad

Amman ○

Cairo ○

Kabul ○

Islamabad ▲

●	Stopover points
■	Staging points
▲	Pick-up points
○	Detainee transfer / drop-off points

0   km   1500

war rules, and a nonstate global organization that is not bound to follow these rules, has raised the issue of the legal status of prisoners of war. The Geneva Conventions that codify the rules of interstate war provide certain human rights protections for prisoners of war that captor states are expected to uphold. After 2001, the Bush administration claimed that persons picked up in the Global War on Terror are not entitled to the legal protections granted by the Geneva Conventions since they do not belong to the regular army of another state. Instead, the Bush administration has labeled them "unlawful enemy combatants," a designation that places these prisoners outside the jurisdiction of U.S. and international law. This has allowed their indeterminate detention without civil rights and independent judiciary oversight (Gregory 2004, 2007).

Geographically, this policy has resulted in a global archipelago of U.S. military and CIA detention centers extending from Bagram, Afghanistan; to Abu Ghraib, Iraq; to Guantanamo, Cuba. Among these, the saga of the Guantanamo Bay prison stands out because of the spatial logic used to select this site as the location of the main detention center in the Global War on Terror (Gregory 2006). Guantanamo Bay is the site of a U.S. Naval Base in Cuba that enjoys an ambiguous legal status. The territory has been under complete U.S. authority since 1903, but Cuba has retained ultimate sovereignty rights. Prisoners held at Guantanamo Bay are technically outside U.S. state borders and are thus outside the jurisdiction of U.S. federal courts that have the obligation to uphold human rights. In the minds of the Bush administration, this location relieved them from the responsibilities of state sovereignty despite the fact that the detainees were under effective control of the U.S. government. The first detainees arrived at Guantanamo in 2002, and soon the prison became synonymous with U.S. human rights abuses in the Global War on Terror. Guantanamo Bay is an example of how the U.S. government attempted to transcend the limitations of its own territorial borders to deal with transnational terrorism in ways it deemed appropriate at the time. The irony is that, at the same time, the same government was busy reinforcing those same borders, presenting them to the public as the ultimate protection against transnational terrorism.

"Extraordinary rendition" is another practice that has shaped the geography of the U.S. Global War on Terror. It implies clandestine operations to kidnap terrorist suspects and transfer them across borders to secret interrogation sites in other states where they can face torture (Gregory 2007). No formal records of these detainees are kept. Officially, they do not exist. Although this practice is illegal under U.S. law, it has been widely used after 2001 in the U.S. Global War on Terror. However, given its illegal nature, the procedure has never been explicitly acknowledged by government officials.

The purpose of "extraordinary rendition" is to keep detainees outside the reach of law by circumventing state borders. This is accomplished by implementing a complex geographical infrastructure to allow covert movement through state borders. Such infrastructure can include CIA-operated secret detention sites in foreign countries as well as in the United States, detention centers in various countries operated by local intelligence services, surveillance centers, transfer sites, and flight routes served by civilian aircraft to avoid suspicion (Marty 2006). These are all tied together operationally in a way that closely resembles transnational networks (see figure 3.1 on pages 62 and 73). In this light, extraordinary rendition practices reveal how state actors themselves are becoming more networklike in their actions in order to overcome the territorial restrictions imposed on them by border lines.

The issues discussed in this chapter illustrate several ways in which the territorial overlap between state sovereignty and the organization of social relations has become unsustainable in the circumstances of globalization. There are other forces, situated at spatial scales other than the state, that impact people's lives. State border lines do not provide a sufficiently effective framework for addressing some of the major issues affecting twenty-first-century societies. The territorial scope of these issues requires that they be regulated by different types of borders. The next chapter will examine how this process of border change works and what outcome it is producing.

4

Producing Global
Border Spaces

BORDER-MAKING DILEMMAS
IN THE TWENTY-FIRST CENTURY

Global flows have unsettled the grid of nation-state borders as the preeminent political, economic, and cultural division of the world. The central questions that emerge now are, What is the future of state borders, and what will this future look like? Will state border lines disappear altogether? Will they be replaced by functional borders or by social boundaries? Will they regain their preeminent status? Who will make the new borders? What shape will they take? How will they function? This chapter engages with these questions to provide a path for understanding the influence that state borders may have on peoples' future lives.

The production of border spaces in the era of globalization is driven by the demands of quick and dependable spatial mobility on the one hand and tangible societal and personal security on the other. The former has found expression in the "open borders" discourse, while the latter has come to be known as the "border securitization" discourse. All major border regimes in the early twenty-first century are actively shaped at the encounter between these two discourses. Of particular interest here are the territorial outcomes these discourses are producing with regard to bordering practices and processes.

It is important to realize that contemporary bordering dilemmas are not inescapable. The need for territorial borders to reconcile mobility with security is not the only possible response to changes introduced by globalization. For the most part, the current issues emerge out of efforts to preserve the nation-state as the dominant form of territorial organization of social relations. Borders may play significantly different roles in mediating between security and mobility if alternative modes of territorial organization are considered.

At the core of the debate are two broad sets of contradictions generated by current trends in globalization. First, there is a geopolitical contradiction between the localized scope of national governments and the need for global governance. Second, there is a geoeconomic contradiction between the neoliberal economic practices that accentuate unequal global development and the need for sustainable and equitable global development. The "open borders" and "border securitization" discourses are outcomes of this "battle of globalization versus globalization," as David Newman has called it (2006b, 182). When borders open, not all social groups and all places stand to benefit in equal measure. In both developed and developing countries, some groups may reap clear economic and political benefits, while others may bear the brunt of the costs. The groups that find themselves at a disadvantage may choose to fight back by demanding the "securitization" of borders.

The idea that reasserting strict control over state borders can restore the previous order is a problematic one because it casts spatial mobility and security in contradictory terms. This view creates a false choice between mobility and security (Lyon 2007b) that hinders finding innovative solutions for reconciling the territorial logics of movement and spatial rigidity. Initially, the economically inspired "open borders" discourse dominated the debate regarding the role of state borders in globalization. During the last decade, the emphasis has shifted, and the politically and culturally inspired "border securitization" discourse has become the main driving force behind contemporary bordering processes (Andreas 2003; Newman 2006b). However, the realities of globalization make the closing of borders a highly unattractive option, as this course of action can potentially destabilize even the most powerful of states. Under these circumstances, the "border securitization" discourse aims less to physically close borders and more to enhance the *selectivity* of borders.

Viewed in terms of degrees of permeability, the mobility-security debate seems to be transcended. Selective permeability has gone hand in hand with border opening from the beginning. Selected classes of people and goods have been allowed unrestricted movement across borders, while others were banned. Border securitization seems poised to tighten control over movement across borders but not to sever it (Sparke 2006). State borders are expected to function much like a selective membrane or filter, with variable degrees of porosity; they may be porous for most forms of capital but not for most categories of unskilled labor (Anderson and O'Dowd 1999). In keeping up with the information age, borders have recently been likened to "firewalls" designed to allow the smooth functioning of legitimate traffic while blocking unwanted intruders (Walters 2006a). The key question that emerges here is who decides what constitutes legitimate traffic? Moreover, how can one be confident that one's own mobility, taken for granted as legitimate today, will not be deemed illegitimate tomorrow?

A global border regime of highly selective permeability would appear to enable the coexistence of territorially bounded nation-states with global flows. However, border securitization in a world of flows is easier said than done. This goal has placed state borders in a paradoxical situation: they have to allow uninhibited cross-border flows while retaining effective territorial protection capabilities. Put differently, fixed border lines have the task of reconciling the contradictory spatial logics of mobility and territorial security (Brunet-Jailly 2007). Evidence suggests that border lines make a poor fix for such a task. The problem is that state border lines have been designed for purposes that reflect the social, economic, and political realities of the nineteenth century, which were markedly different from the ones of the twenty-first century.

To this end, we are currently witnessing the emergence of complementary forms of state borders and bordering practices that evade the norms of territorial linearity and are better adapted to the networked geography of globalization. This diversification of the spatial shape assumed by borders appears to provide the latest avenue for transcending contemporary bordering dilemmas and points to the emergence of a plurality of border types. At the same time, this context also brings to the fore the issue of the social costs associated with the new bordering practices, as new ways for bringing these borders under democratic control still remain to be found.

UNTANGLING DE/RETERRITORIALIZATION AND DE/REBORDERING

Deterritorialization and reterritorialization, as well as debordering and rebordering processes, are spatial manifestations of contemporary changes occurring in the territorial organization of social life. Deterritorialization and reterritorialization are concepts commonly associated with poststructuralism and postmodernism. They were initially developed by the French social theorists Gilles Deleuze and Felix Guattari (1977) to illustrate how the dynamic interaction between capitalism, power, and identity constantly define and redefine social structures and processes. Border studies have employed these concepts to capture the complex issues emerging from the encounter between state border lines and global flows.

Deterritorialization implies social relations escaping the straitjacket of state territoriality mainly by overcoming the container role state territories have played during the modern era. Debordering primarily implies the disappearance of the barrier role of the border in its capacity of the container's wall, or even the disappearance of the border itself. The latter is meant more specifically, focusing on the functions and geography of the state border proper, while the former refers to the broader territory of the state. Nonetheless, deterritorialization and debordering are not seen here as separate processes, as it is difficult in practice to have one without the other. Territories become identifiable through their borders. Thus, the deterritorialization of social relations implies the removal of territorial barriers and vice versa.

Likewise, reterritorialization and rebordering are related concepts. The former generally implies a restructuring of the modern territorial framework of organization of social life, leading to the emergence of new territorial assemblages of social relations transcending the scope and the scale of the nation-state (Brenner 1999a, 1999b; Popescu 2008; Sassen 2006; Toal 1999). The latter suggests the reemergence of the barrier role of borders or the erection of new borders (Andreas 2003). It is important to underline that rebordering is not only about the reinforcement of existing state borders, but also about different ways of bordering that include new types of borders and new border functions (Walters 2002, 2006a).

Deterritorialization and Debordering

Deterritorialization and debordering are normally associated with globalization to suggest that globalization pressures have loosened the bonds that tied economics, politics, and culture to fixed spatial configurations such as national territories. In a broader sense this situation indicates a decrease in the significance of national territory and borders for social life, thus unraveling territoriality as it has been constructed during the modern era (Sassen 2006; Toal 1999). Globalization flows, suggesting borderless mobility, are perceived as replacing the space of places of the nation-state, which entailed bounded territoriality. It appears that a primarily networked organization of power is replacing a primarily territorial organization of power (Castells 2000). This opens up the possibility of people living as nodes in a network society that stretches over the globe rather than in national societies delineated by territorial borders.

Specifically, deterritorialization and debordering processes take aim at the global system of sovereign nation-states that have dominated the territorial organization of power during the modern era. Nation-states are devolving some of their exclusive powers on at least three main geographical scales: upward to the supranational bodies such as the EU, the North American Free Trade Agreement (NAFTA), and the IMF; downward to subnational institutions such as regional governments, local

councils, and development agencies; and sideways to an array of transnational and private organizations (J. Anderson 1996; Blatter 2001; Brenner
1999a). Overlapping and intersecting national, regional, supranational,
transnational, and private power structures that fulfill the basic needs
of the people appear to render obsolete the traditional source of state
power that Mann (1984) located in the state's unique capacity to provide
territorially centralized services to its citizens. These evolutions signal
novel possibilities for the spatial organization of social relations along
functional rather than territorial lines according to which specific regulation regimes manage specific fields of activity across national territories.

The most noticeable early development underscoring the contemporary interstate border regime has consisted in an overall opening of borders in the sense of ease of crossing and a departure from hard national
borders. It is this sense that the term *debordering* is meant to capture. There
has been a gradual denationalization of border functions to the point that
they are not predominantly inward looking, and they do not exclusively
revolve around the national domain, as Sassen (2006) compellingly ar-
gues. With globalization, numerous border functions are increasingly
outwardly redirected to facilitate interconnection. Borders have not dissolved, but they have become increasingly permeable to allow rapid and
sustained cross-border exchanges (Newman 2006b). While this is not an
even process across the globe, the liberalization of the border-crossing regime has been implemented in all major regions of the world (Perkmann
and Sum 2002).

From a political economy perspective, these deterritorialization and
debordering processes are understood in terms of the spatial characteristics of successive rounds of capital accumulation. If the previous
strategies of capital accumulation largely took place at the scale of
national markets, the current ones favor global markets (Harvey 2000).
Financial flows circle the globe at dazzling speeds via digital telecommunications networks, creating massive amounts of wealth (Warf and
Purcell 2001). An entire offshore global economy has emerged, anchored
in an archipelago of offshore centers that provide tax shelters for TNC
financing schemes and other banking activities (Palan 2006; Warf 2002).
Manufacturing and service firms have adopted truly global production
models that involve an integrated network of places and just-in-time
production systems. They are outsourcing jobs from developed to
developing economies as part of a strategy to compete in global-scale
markets. Moreover, national governments themselves have carved up
"special economic zones" inside the territories of their states. These offer a host of local incentives to attract foreign investment and amount to
an attempt by national governments to overcome the regulatory functions of their own national borders (Park 2005). Developments such as

these have unsettled national controls over national economies and have made state borders appear increasingly archaic.

Cross-cultural exchanges across state borders have soared with globalization as well. Cultural and social issues are increasingly playing out in the global arena, rather than within state borders (Appadurai 1996). Numerous governmental social policies and executive functions have been privatized, indicating a spatial shift from hierarchical government to networked governance. Migration flows and information technologies have created transnational networks of diasporic communities and have reinvigorated local and regional identities that are now enacted globally (Leitner and Ehrkamp 2006). People can communicate across borders with more ease today and in more direct and personal ways via a large variety of information technology mediums, including e-mail, video messengers, chat rooms, Web blogs, and social networking sites like Facebook and YouTube (Boid 2010; Longan and Purcell 2011).

Geopolitically, during the last two decades the world political map has seen dramatic developments that have dismantled a world order that appeared timeless (Toal 1999). Some well-established sovereign states like Czechoslovakia and Yugoslavia have fragmented or disappeared altogether, while new ones like Belarus and East Timor have emerged. The militarization of borders has been scaled back in various regions of the world, as illustrated by the dismantling of border fences and other military fortifications, by de-mining efforts, and by replacing military border guards with police units. The lines between the domestic and the foreign realms of politics have blurred as central governments face increasing difficulties in managing crisis situations that often acquire transnational dimensions. Increasingly there is a measure of internationalization in politics and crisis management that appears to diminish the sovereign power of the state.

Some authors have interpreted these deterritorialization and debordering instances as the "end of geography" and the emergence of a borderless world, in the sense that territoriality and territorial lines will be of little consequence to social life in the future (O'Brian 1992; Ohmae 1990). In this view, deterritorialization and debordering are unstoppable phenomena leading to nonterritorial and borderless social relations and the demise of the nation-state. Such a unidirectional understanding of globalization has poor explanatory power for the complex changes under way in bordering processes. The core fallacy of the borderless-world thesis consists in its reliance on Cartesian understandings of space as a rigid entity that can be sliced into precise pieces and then rendered meaningful with the help of mathematics (Elden 2005a). This perspective assumes that if one shape is destabilized and becomes nonquantifiable, then it has disappeared and can be replaced only by another shape with quantifiable features. Thus, the possibility of coexistence, overlapping, and hybridity is precluded. According to this logic, when the underlining assumptions about the linearity of state borders are shaken by transnational phenomena, it means that borders are expected to fade away and be replaced by global flows. The national scale has to disappear for the global one to emerge.

There are two main reasons why deterritorialization and debordering should not be overstated. First, social relations cannot simply lose territoriality altogether, as society needs to relate somehow to territory. Rather, it is more appropriate to speak of social relations evading a particular mode of territorial organization. The new assemblages of power that are being created continue to use territoriality and borders as modes of organization and control, albeit under new configurations. Global flows display territoriality and borders as well. Their geography of nodes and links suggests the increasing importance of place to the organization of social relations. Swyngedouw (1997) called this process "glocalization" (rather than globalization) precisely to underline the emerging intimate connections between global flows and local places. Second, we cannot even speak with confidence of state territoriality and borders losing their appeal, as new territorial states continue to appear. The USSR did indeed deterritorialize, and its borders disappeared, only for the space it occupied to be reterritorialized and rebordered again in new states.

We can speak of deterritorialization and debordering only to invoke reterritorialization and rebordering. Deterritorialization and reterritorialization as well as debordering and rebordering are best understood as processes that unfold simultaneously. They are mutually constitutive processes (Sparke 2005). Some spaces can experience debordering while others may experience rebordering, or the same space may experience both of these processes at the same time. Social relations do not completely lose their territorial grounding and their boundaries before they reterritorialize. Rather, social relations acquire other territorial configurations and boundaries even as they lose their previous ones. This means that the new border spaces, while qualitatively different, will include vestiges of the old (Toal 1996, 1999).

Reterritorialization and Rebordering

Globalization can be understood in terms of reterritorialization and rebordering dynamics (Brenner 1999a, 1999b). Evidence suggests that globalization has not led to ceaseless deterritorialization and debordering. Geography has not ended, the nation-state did not fade away, and the world has not become borderless. Rather, geography is being reorganized, and borders are acquiring new significance and new roles. Globalization has created conditions for the spatial reconfiguration and rebordering of social relations in a way that transcends the territorial framework of the nation-state system and the grid of territorial borders associated with it (Agnew 2009; Sassen 2006; Sparke 2005). Now the task is to understand what new border spaces are emerging and how.

An examination of the current bordering dynamics has to start with the recognition that the global reach of the nation-state system means that globalization flows necessarily have to engage with territorial states and their borders. Globalization flows touch down in various geographical places that serve as territorial anchors, such as global cities and resource-rich regions. The result is that flows become embedded in territories, and in their turn territories become embedded in flows (Axford 2006; Dicken et al. 2001). It is here, at this junction, where global flows meet territorial states, that reterritorialization and rebordering happens.

Digital information technologies such as the Internet have been generally viewed as the most borderless of technologies. Indeed, the Internet's potential to transcend state borders and undermine a government's monopoly over information is unprecedented. However, uneven access to the Internet worldwide (also known as "the digital divide ") generated by immense disparities in wealth between developed and developing countries, as well as within them, constitutes barriers as formidable as well-guarded territorial borders (Warf 2001). Moreover, what is often overlooked in accounts of borderless information technologies is the fact that they rely on an infrastructure composed of providers, routing servers, and consumers that are very much grounded in territory and are thus open to state regulation (Eriksson and Giacomello 2009).

The case of the Chinese government (as well as of several Middle Eastern governments), which has managed to regulate domestic Internet content, is a prime example of rebordering in a seemingly borderless information age (Warf 2010). The desire of large Internet providers such as Yahoo, Google, and others to penetrate the Chinese market led them to bow to the Chinese government's demands for censorship and to relinquish exclusive control over key privacy aspects of this technology. Generally this has involved Google or Yahoo censoring their Internet services in China by blocking specific words on their search engines and websites that the Chinese authorities have deemed undesirable. In more extreme cases, the rebordering of the Internet has allowed the Chinese authorities to identify political dissidents and imprison them, as illustrated by the revelations that Yahoo has repeatedly disclosed the personal e-mail information of Chinese dissidents to the Chinese authorities (Macartney 2006).

In finance, territorial borders may do little to control electronic money flows, but national governments do play a role in regulating global financial markets by stretching certain aspects of their regulatory borders on a global scale. One recent example is the effort by developed-world governments together with multilateral and supranational organizations such as the Organisation for Economic Cooperation and Development (OECD), the IMF, and the EU to regulate offshore financial centers to curb tax evasion practices (Maurer 2008). The manner in which this is done, by pressuring offshore centers to comply with U.S. or EU tax codes, indicates the emergence of a global regime of financial norms that is in part autonomous and in part state controlled.

The worldwide economic recession at the end of the first decade of the twenty-first century presents new opportunities to examine reterritorialization and rebordering processes at work. With the global financial system in a state of shock and numerous manufacturing TNCs on the verge of bankruptcy, the state emerged as the only institution with enough political and economic clout to turn to for rescue. Global flows of all sorts had to be bailed out by the territorial state at taxpayers' expense, which demonstrates the codependent relationship that exists between transnational flows and the territorial state. If the bailout had not happened, the state would have suffered unprecedented destabilization. Of utmost importance here is that the economic recovery plans put in place throughout 2009 and 2010 have been *national* plans designed to salvage the *national* economies. All developed states have bailed out corporations headquartered inside their borders. There has been no *global* recovery plan despite the transnational nature of the crisis. However, for the poorer countries that could not come up with bailout money on their own, the IMF has been entrusted to perform such services. This is as close to *global* action as the recovery plans have come.

Moreover, calls for provisions such as "Buy American" to be attached to the U.S. bailout plan reflect broader concerns about the outsourcing of jobs in the developed world and point once again to rebordering tendencies. Such provisions create the illusion that U.S. borders can be used to restore a lost sense of economic security among U.S. citizens, while overlooking the fact that job creation in most U.S. businesses depends to a large extent on cross-border trade linkages. Solutions to global issues such as outsourcing are often rhetorically sought by retrenching behind national borders instead of by seeking to build global regulation regimes that are able to address the root problems across state borders. For example, a global minimum wage and global environmental regulations might go a long way toward addressing outsourcing and other associated issues. Many people across the developed world flock to supermarket chains such as Walmart to buy cheap goods produced by overseas cheap labor, but then they are surprised when their jobs are shipped across borders as well. In other words, many people remain mentally trapped inside state territorial borders, unable to see how their material well-being is increasingly dependent on the ability of national businesses to cross state borders, and how this has hidden costs that the consumer ultimately has to pay as long as her or his livelihood remains circumscribed by state borders. State territorial borders are unable to allow unfettered cross-border flows and to protect against their outcomes at the same time.

In global politics, the end of the Cold War bipolar world order has not led to the disappearance of territorial power politics and the appearance of a more peaceful world. The emergence of new geopolitical actors along with the United States, such as the European Union, China, Russia, and other smaller regional powers, indicates the persistence of territorial power politics. During the last decade alone, the United States invaded Afghanistan and Iraq, Russia has been busy rebuilding its sphere of influence in the former Soviet Union, the European Union has expanded its influence in its eastern and southern neighborhoods, China is inserting itself into Southeast Asia and Africa, and Iran has embarked on a path to acquire nuclear weapons.

The emerging picture of the current moment of globalization suggests that bordering as a principle of organization of social relations is far from disappearing. Some identities may be enacted at a global scale today, but the emergence of new ethnic and territorial identities points to the salience of territorial borders as cultural markers. Territorial borders have lost some of their previous functions, but they have also gained new ones. They are not fading away, but they are being reinvented. At the same time, rebordering processes should not be simplistically interpreted as signaling the emergence of a closed-border regime in which closed borders are replacing open borders. Current border realities defy such a model of reasoning (Paasi 2009; Rumford 2006a). De- and rebordering processes cannot be adequately conceived in terms of binary oppositions such as open and closed borders, as these can be mutually constitutive—what is experienced by some as a closed border can be experienced as an open border by others (Newman 2006a). The current direction of border change can be better captured by thinking in terms of the reterritorialization of borders and their functions.

The nation-state, in its quest to remain relevant in the twenty-first century, plays an active role in the twin processes of deterritorialization/reterritorialization and debordering/rebordering. The nation-state remains the basic geographical framework within and through which the production of new assemblages of territorial order and their borders takes place (Brenner 1999a). The relocation of state powers to the sub- and supranational levels and to private organizations does not necessarily mean the end of state sovereignty. Instead, the nature of sovereignty has changed in the sense that it has been denationalized and does not exclusively match territorially fixed state borders (Agnew 2009; Sassen 1999). This transformation signals the emergence of a new global architecture of territorial power with multiscalar and overlapping sovereignties that are shared between territorial states and nonstate structures wielding territorial power such as global cities, TNCs, supranational organizations, transnational social networks, and subnational regions (J. Anderson 1996; A. Murphy 1999; Sassen 2006). The result is a combination of reorganized and rescaled fixed political territories on the one hand, and mobile power structures that remain territorially grounded in various ways on the other hand. Such reterritorialized order represents more than the rearrangement of territorial borders across scales, as Cartesian logic would have it, with nation-state borders being replaced by supra- and subnational borders. Rather, contemporary reterritorialization includes interscalar and functional-territorial power structures combining and recombining to form territorial assemblages with borders that are unstable in time and incomplete in space.

It remains an open question whether this new architecture of territorial order will be a lasting one, or if it represents a transition stage to a new coherent territorial system with more stable borders. The tendency of states to coalesce into supranational trading blocs with their own territorial borders, such as the EU, NAFTA, the Association of Southeast Asian Nations (ASEAN), and Mercosur, suggests the latter, while global trade, the diffusion of information technology, and the formation of diaspora networks suggest the former. What is apparent today is that reterritorialization and rebordering are increasing the complexity of bordering processes, leading to radical transformations in the nature, the spatiality, the meaning, and the functions of state borders.

THE GEOGRAPHY OF BORDER SPACES

One of the most significant impacts that rebordering and reterritorialization processes have on the geography of interstate borders is to move attention beyond territorial border lines. This change implies the shift of focus from borders as territorially fixed locations to more territorially fluid borders, which are able to assume multiple and changing locations (Arbaret-Schulz et al. 2004; Walters 2004). These developments have been associated with an unprecedented multiplication, diversification, specialization, and personalization of borders. There are now more borders to be crossed in more places and of more kinds than ever before—supranational borders, regional borders, metropolitan borders, special-purpose district borders, free economic zone borders, gated community private borders, and the borders of transnational networks.

There are three main spatial directions along which bordering takes place within the emerging global border regimes—borderlands, networked borders, and border lines. These spatial contexts for bordering are not mutually exclusive and should be understood in conjunction, as they can occur simultaneously in the same geographical setting. Networked borders and border lines can be found in borderlands, and vice versa. Moreover, borderlands and networked borders have not replaced border lines when it comes to state territorial limits. Formally, state borders continue to remain lines. However, for many practical purposes, the performance of border functions does not display a territorially linear pattern anymore. Formal claims to linear state borders are being transformed by globalization realities.

Borderlands

The view of borders as borderlands recuperates a sense of space that has always characterized state borders despite their formal linear understanding during the twentieth century. Seeing borders as spaces rather than lines acknowledges that the realities created by border making cannot be adequately made sense of by imagining borders in nonspatial ways. Borderlands are not rigid spaces. They display large variation in size according to the intensity and type of cross-border exchanges, the nature of the border regime that governs them, the center-periphery relationships inside the state they belong to, and the territorial scale of analysis (Morehouse 2004; Paasi 1996). Under these circumstances, borderlands can range anywhere from narrow strips of land adjacent to the border line, to large regions like the U.S.-Mexico borderland or Pakistan's Northwest Territories, to entire countries, as in the case of Afghanistan or Moldova.

These borderlands are not abstract spaces. They are spaces where people live, spaces inhabited by real people living daily lives (Paasi 1996), in contrast to border lines that can only be inhabited by people's imagination of what borders should be about. Borderlands blur the strict sense of separation between inside and outside that border lines imply. Their spatiality makes it easier to see that there are two sides to a border and that this entire space has to be considered when dealing with bordering processes (see figure 4.1). Borderlands reveal a more gradual transition in space from one state territory to another, rather than a sharp and swift encounter as border lines would have it.

Borderlands came into being in various ways as a direct consequence of border making. Most are not the outcome of peaceful processes but of events such as wars, mass killings, and forced population changes, and they are often still contested (Forsberg 1995; Rumley and Minghi 1991). In some cases they resulted from the division of self-aware regions between nation-states, creating ethnic minorities on both sides of the border, while in other cases they became borderlands after the formation of national

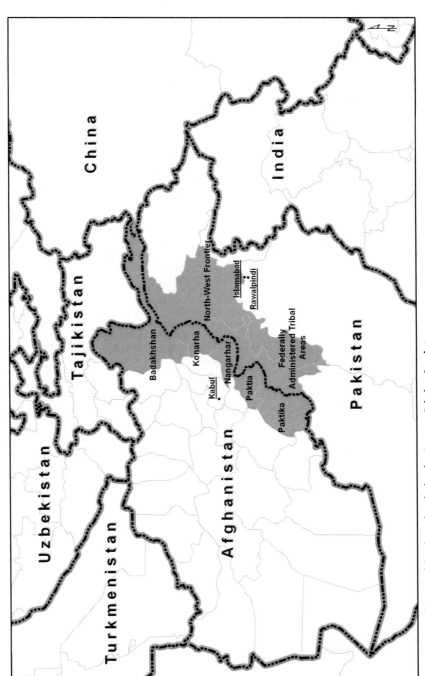

Figure 4.1   Pakistan-Afghanistan borderlands. *Source:* Cristina Scarlat.

states because of their position at the confines of the new system of national organization. In circumstances where these borderlands have been
less successfully integrated into the nation-state, they have been typically
relegated to a subordinate status that has created their image of enduring
peripheries (Jonsson et al. 2000; A. Murphy 1993).

The centralization of power in core regions and capital cities that charac-
terizes nation-states has contributed to borderlands becoming "the objects
rather than the subjects of policies and politics" (Anderson and O'Dowd
1999, 597). As modern territorial sovereignty is normally asserted and
defended at the borders, governments tend to focus predominantly on
the political and military aspects of borderlands and less on their social
and economic aspects. Development strategies regarding these areas
have generally been less sensitive to the interests of borderland inhabitants, especially in circumstances in which relations with neighbor states
were tense. This situation has rendered border regions economically peripheral. Additionally, where ethnic minorities inhabit borderlands, they
tend to become cultural peripheries as well. As a result, borderlands can
become places where multiple conflicts accumulate, which reinforce their
image as peripheries. Nonetheless, in contrast to this image in a national
context, borderlands can occupy central positions at the supranational
level. For example, they may be located close to core resource areas in
neighboring states or along transcontinental transportation corridors that
have the potential to benefit the development of borderlands.

Borderlands are not easily recognizable spaces at first glance. Road
signs rarely announce their beginning. However, their landscapes and
the social relations that shape them are peculiar, setting them apart from
the rest of the territory of the state. The typical borderland image includes fences, watchtowers, customs houses, border guards, and military
infrastructure. In addition to this, we can also speak of a multitude of
other landscapes. There is a social landscape, with controlled population
movement, special settlement policies, smuggling networks, and facilities
for cross-border travel not available to the rest of the state's population.
There is an economic landscape that includes transportation hubs with
railroad and bus depots, trucking centers, warehouses, free zones, and
export-oriented factories and farms. There is a political and institutional
landscape, with regional political parties, consulates, detention centers
for immigrants, and NGOs assisting refugees. A cultural landscape is
also identifiable, with monuments and museums of national importance,
bilingual street signs, ethnic minority centers, and a variety of languages
spoken in the street.

All these characteristics, along with many others, make up the fabric of
borderlands. They reveal a meeting place, a place of contact, confluence,
and hybridity that mediates passage from one side to the other (Amilhat-

Szary and Fourny 2006; Kramsch 2007; Newman 2006a; Pavlakovich-Kochi et al. 2004; Rumford 2008a). These circumstances suggest that borderlands are spaces that can enable living across borders, rather than living inside borders. In turn, imagining living in a state of permanent border-crossing allows us to understand the formation of identities defined by belonging to multiple places and national cultures. It is in this light that borderlands emerge as in-between spaces, transitional spaces that can serve to smooth over differences and facilitate interaction. Such borderland qualities have allowed many stakeholders to see state borders as potential resources that can be used as gateways and bridges, thus as spaces that connect rather than separate (O'Dowd 2002b; Perkmann 2007a). These views have helped transform perceptions of borderlands from being peripheral to central in many places that have experienced relatively permeable border regimes. Borderlands occupy now-prominent positions in development strategies crafted by numerous decision makers involved in regional and supranational integration. These themes will be addressed further in chapter 6.

At the same time, the in-betweenness or transitionality of borderlands can also mean that they continue to be perceived as no-man's lands, spaces of exception where anything goes (R. Jones 2009a). The image of borderlands as buffer zones and shatter belts that absorb the negative energy between states has not disappeared, as exemplified by the existence of the Demilitarized Zone on the Korean peninsula and by the Pakistani government's compliance with U.S. bombing of its frontier territories.

Networked Borders

Seeing borders in terms of networks is a relatively recent development that builds on the work of Etienne Balibar, who has written on the dispersal of contemporary borders and their functions from the margins of the state territory to a multitude of locations in the interior (2002, 2004). This argument, also known as "borders are everywhere," has led some border scholars to develop parallels between the characteristics of networks and flows and those of recent border-making processes (Amoore 2006; Axford 2006; Delanty 2006; Rumford 2006a, 2006b, 2007, 2008a; Walters 2002, 2006a). Walters (2004, 2006a) and Rumford (2006a, 2006b) have both captured the spatial nature of these border-making developments by calling them "networked borders." By this, these scholars mean that borders have been dispersed throughout societies and re-created in a network form spanning multiple states and even the entire globe.

Viewing borders as networks allows them to transcend the territorial rigidity of border lines. If borderlands infuse borders with a sense of space by giving them an area, then networks give borders their spatial mobility. Borders can be disembedded from their local contexts, projected at distance, and then implanted anywhere in the state territory (Balibar 2004). Such "portability" of borders changes the way movement through space is organized and how people and places come into contact. The node-and-link territoriality of networked borders brings people and places together by connecting them directly across space, unlike modern state border territoriality that connects them via contiguous state territories. This situation opens up the entire space of the globe to bordering processes, thus accelerating the proliferation of borders and multiplying the actors involved in their establishment. The implications for society of such novel territoriality of borders are paramount and will be discussed in depth in the next chapter.

Of utmost importance here is that networked borders appear to provide an optimal solution to the dilemma of open borders versus security that bedevils the current round of globalization. The main idea behind networked borders is to check people and goods before they reach the state border proper. Performing border functions away from the state border lines allows borders to travel with the flows. In other words, the border becomes embedded in the flow (Axford 2006; Sassen 2006). Hence flows can potentially be scrutinized along the entire journey from the point of origin to the point of arrival. Technically, these developments are rendering territorially linear borders redundant. At most, state border lines can be seen as supplemental checking stations along the way, much like nodes (of linear morphology indeed) in a wider, global network of border networks. This realignment of the relationship between borders and territory—from territorial rigidity to mobility—makes it more effective for securing mobility in a global world, thus achieving a highly selective permeability of borders. In the end, networked borders indicate the adaptation of the ordering capacity of borders to a world of flows. It appears that, for the moment, it is only by disembedding, multiplying, and dispersing borders that globalization can be made sustainable while preserving the nation-state and its claims to territorial sovereignty. Thus a global world will not be one without borders, as many have hoped. Instead, it will be one that has globalized borders.

At least three interconnected spatial dimensions attest to the nonlinear territoriality of networked borders. First, there is an *outward* orientation in the case of the presence of border control aspects from one country inside the territory of another (Collyer 2008; Walters 2006a). Second, there is an *inward* dimension that emerges from domestic aspects of border management (Coleman 2007a; Paasi 1996; Vaughan-Williams 2008). Third, there is an *in-between* dimension revealed by the incorporation of places with uncertain politico-legal status into border-making strategies (Hyndman and Mountz 2007). Numerous components of these dimensions intersect in myriad ways to form a web of borders that has achieved global reach.

Any attempt to map the territoriality of networked borders can only be partial given the fact that they are incipient and change configuration often. Still, the value of a mapping exercise consists in revealing that there is little resemblance between the rhizomatic geography of networked borders and the habitual gridlike one of state borders. The following description of the legend of such a map is by no means either fixed or complete. First, networked borders are encountered abroad, such as in consulates and embassies where visas are issued. Second, they are found in locations such as airports, ports, bus and train stations, and travel agencies, where travel documents are checked (Walters 2002). Third, they are found on the seas, where law enforcement crews patrol offshore waters to prevent refugees from reaching the beaches of southern Florida, the Spanish Canary Islands, northern Australia, or southern Italy (Ferrer-Gallardo 2008). Fourth, they are found in a myriad of places inland where people's identities are verified, at hotels, Internet cafés, police stations, supermarket parking lots, street corners, and on highways (Coleman 2005; Rumford 2006a). Fifth, they are visible in the form of gated communities and zoning policies used to segregate people in space (van Houtum 2002; Walters 2006a). Sixth, we notice them in the in-between places where people's status is purposefully kept undetermined, such as refugee camps, immigration detention centers, Guantanamo Bay, and others (Mountz 2011). Seventh, they are found in public institutions (Lahav and Guiraudon 2000; Paasi 1996), in places such as courthouses, hospitals, schools, and driver's license offices, as well as in private businesses at meatpacking plants, construction sites, and strawberry fields. Eighth, they can be found in trucking centers and warehouses where goods are moved around. Ninth, they can be found online, in software that upholds intellectual property rights or in software that prescreens personal identity when purchasing airplane tickets (Sassen 2006).

Some of these networked elements of border control are indeed not new. Visa-issuing consulates, refugee camps, and immigration triage centers such as Ellis Island, as well as inland customs offices and immigration enforcement, can be traced back at least to the period after World War I (Walters 2002). However, these were generally fragmented, irregular, and disconnected. What sets contemporary networked borders apart is their generalization, routine, and systemic integration to form a comprehensive border regime of movement control.

The nonlinear territoriality of networked borders has often been mistakenly taken as nonterritoriality. Their scattered territorial nature makes them less visible and creates the illusion that they are disconnected from territory and much easier to cross. Networked borders tend to appear territorially inconspicuous and detached from the rigorous hierarchy of political borders. As a result, many people feel that the physicality of borders has diminished, although they encounter borders more often in their daily lives (Rumford 2006a). In fact, what has changed are the terms of the spatial encounter with borders, as well as the nature of the border-crossing experience. Social and economic categories like race, class, ethnicity, religion, education, wealth, and others have become much more important bordering factors now. These factors affect different groups in different ways at different times and are not easily associated with the archetypical image of borders that most people bear in their minds. Nonetheless, such changes do not make borders nonterritorial. Rather, socioeconomic boundaries and territorial borders are *folded into* each other. Both socioeconomic categories and territoriality come together in networked borders.

For example, passport control at state border lines is typically geographically and socially undifferentiated. While some groups may be treated in a different way than others (e.g., separate customs lines for citizens and noncitizens), everybody has to go through border control at the checkpoint. Consider now the examples of an immigration raid in a neighborhood somewhere in a European city, an impromptu immigration check on a highway near the U.S.-Mexico border, and a visa-issuing office in a consulate in a developing country in Africa. Some people in the neighborhood will have their documents verified while others will not, based perhaps on their physical appearance; some cars on the highway will be waved on while others will be stopped, depending on their type and condition; and some people at the consulate will quickly receive a visa while others will be required to bring additional documentation, possibly to prove their material well-being. All of these decisions create different experiences of crossing *territorial* state borders (even if not in their linear form) based on peoples' physical and socioeconomic characteristics. Accordingly, some groups of people will not see a state border in the middle of a neighborhood, a highway, or a building, while for others the border is all too real. This differential perception of networked borders is all the more interesting if we think that even the people who were present but did not notice the border in the above examples have in fact been bordered in these events. The border existed for them too. They crossed it, but its territoriality did not have the same effect on them because they had the desirable physical and socioeconomic characteristics at that time. However, this begs the question, what will happen to these people next time when the border-crossing requirements have changed?

Another key attribute of networked borders is their movement-friendly structure that favors sustained mobility across space. This is particularly evident when we compare networks with border lines. However, this general statement—that networked borders are movement friendly—needs to be qualified. At the same time, networked borders can be barriers to movement as well, even if they do not look anything like barbed-wire fences. Access to border networks does not automatically include everybody. Some people are better positioned to take advantage of networks' movement-friendly features, while for some people the same features constitute borders in themselves. In these circumstances, we can speak of "the borders of the networked borders" that have to be crossed in order to gain access to spatial mobility.

For instance, at many U.S. consulates overseas, the entire visa application process has been moved online. The visa application form has to be completed and submitted online, the appointment time is communicated to the applicant online, and fees currently totaling over one hundred U.S. dollars must be paid in a special account via specifically designated local banks that most often have branches only in larger cities. All these steps are required just to be considered for a visa. Additional steps have to be taken to actually have one issued. In appearance, this is an unbiased process, as it is open to everybody irrespective of race, religion, or class. In reality, to partake in this process one needs both access to a computer and the skill to use it, as well as a trip to a larger city if one does not live in a metropolitan area. For large segments of the developing-world population, as well as for many members of minority groups in the developed world, computer ownership and skills are not ubiquitous. In the absence of either of these, one has to pay for the services. This is on top of the visa fee that in many developing countries can amount to the equivalent of a month's salary or more.

These examples reveal the profound structuring effects that networked border territoriality has on mobility, influencing who can and who cannot cross state borders, where, and under what circumstances. People have to cross the borders of the networks before they cross the borders of the state. Put differently, one first has to become a member of various "visa clubs" in order to enjoy the mobility benefits that networked borders can offer. To do this requires that people routinely negotiate borders. This shows that borders of all shapes, linear and nonlinear alike, have become more important to the organization of social life in the twenty-first century.

Border Lines

The appeal of linear borders as social ordering devices has not diminished at the beginning of the twenty-first century. It is true that the diversification of border territoriality has eroded the spatial monopoly over various control aspects that border lines have long enjoyed. At the same time, it is also the case that borderlands and networked borders have developed, for the most part, in addition to border lines rather than instead of them. In many ways, the popularity of linear borders has increased lately, as a growing number of social groups have come to see them in terms of one of the few remaining tools available to protect against neoliberal globalization forces.

This lasting power of border lines is due in part to their familiarity. They provide a simplified blueprint for organizing difference along us-them binary oppositions. Many people continue to consider border lines essential identity markers. Not surprisingly, the symbolic functions of state border lines have retained center stage even as numerous other traditional functions are dispersed. Border lines figure prominently in the discourses of politicians and civil society stakeholders alike. To this end, it is telling that all newly emerged states have insisted on having clearly demarcated border lines. Any other form of territorial borders would be unthinkable. Moreover, when in doubt, states dispute the exact location of the most minuscule segments of their border lines. Equally attesting to the continuing grip that border lines have on peoples' imaginations is the fact that the solution to the sixty-year-old Israel-Palestine conflict, one of the most important current geopolitical hot spots on the planet, is sought in terms of territorial borders to separate the two parties involved.

Three current developments underline the vitality of border lines in the globalization era. First, they continue to emerge at a rate that far outpaces their demise. During the last two decades, more than 26,000 kilometers of new borders have emerged worldwide, with Europe and Asia leading the way (Foucher 2007). To these we can also add the borders of quasi-states and other rebel-held territories that have de facto border lines, such as Transnistria and South Ossetia.

Second, there is a global drive to demarcate the last unclear border line sectors of the planet, no matter how small or remote they may be. This border line compulsion also extends to bodies of water such as rivers and seas. From the Amazonian and Southeast Asian jungles, to the deserts of the Arabian Peninsula and Central Asia, to the cold waters of the Arctic, surveyor teams are busy measuring sharp state border lines with the precision offered by satellite technology. Then they attempt to immortalize these lines in the landscape by building symbolic border markers, often only to have them later removed by the local population or swallowed by water, sand, or jungle. Interestingly, even as a growing number of national governments warm up to the idea of borderlands, it appears that they do so more easily only after the state border lines are securely in place.

Third, an active effort to physically reinforce border lines can be noticed in all major regions of the world. Walling and fencing people in and out of territories has become a major border business and a political panacea. Thousands of miles of border fences, walls, and other barriers have already been built worldwide, from the U.S.-Mexico border to the EU borders in Eastern Europe and North Africa, and from Saudi Arabia and Israel to the India-Bangladesh border (Andreas 2000; Diener and Hagen 2009; R. Jones 2009b). Tens of thousands of kilometers more are in the planning stages (Foucher 2007). Among these, the Israeli separation fence from the Palestinians, the U.S. fence at its border with Mexico, and the fence around the Spanish enclaves of Ceuta and Melilla in Morocco stand out. These are impressive structures, combining several types of barriers to movement such as concrete walls, metal fences, and watchtowers, in some places arranged in double or even triple rows and separated by razor wire or ditches. They are completed by access roads for border guard patrol vehicles. They often include technologically sophisticated equipment such as motion detection sensors, infrared cameras, electronic lighting, and other devices. Although these are not continuous structures, they can extend for hundreds of kilometers and reach over seven meters high (see figures 4.2 and 4.3).

Figure 4.2   The U.S. border fence at its border with Mexico viewed from Montezuma Pass, Arizona. Source: Jussi Laine.

Figure 4.3 **Israeli separation wall between the Israelis and the Palestinians in Jerusalem.** *Source:* **Author.**

Such landscapes are reminiscent of war zones, only there is no war and there are no warring armies. What purpose, then, do border walls serve? What is the existential danger they are supposed to protect against? Are the benefits they bring worth their material, social, and political costs? These questions continue to remain unanswered. It is known that the overall utility of border walls is highly problematic. Despite their multi-billion-dollar price tags, they can be overcome with relative ease by, among other things, scaling them or digging under them. However, their symbolic value is much clearer, its effects running deep into the societies they seek to separate (Andreas 2000). In the absence of an invading army at the border, it is everyday life that these walls are intended to control. In other words, the more benign threat from the poor and the smuggler has replaced the more critical one from the enemy soldier. The story most border walls tell is that wealth and power seek to fence themselves in. Nonetheless, the same story also tells that the poor and the weak seek to get in.

In light of the three border types described above, the map of globalization's borders appears rather crowded as it combines multiple layers of border territoriality. The first one is the layer showing the familiar grid of state border lines; the second shows the networked borders described earlier in this chapter; and the third bears the fuzzy spaces of borderlands. This congested map comes close to representing border spatiality in the era of globalization. While it is unclear how legible this congested map is to the ordinary citizen, one thing it makes clear is that borders are increasingly everywhere.

5

Controlling Mobility

THE SECURITY PARADIGM AND BORDER MAKING

The security function of borders is one of the oldest and most basic. Modern state borders were expected to provide security by facilitating the military defense of territory against external threats such as invasion from other states. The security of the nation was seen in territorially fixed terms as a primarily military and geopolitical issue that revolved around the protection of the institution of the state. To secure the nation was to defend the state's territorial sovereignty. Then it was the task of the state to secure the daily life of the citizen. This division of work reflected the dual outside/inside distinction with which nation-states have long operated (Walker 1993). National security was a matter of external concern and was assumed by the military, while personal security was a matter of domestic concern and was assumed by the police.

Mobility imperatives under globalization have fundamentally altered the security functions state borders have traditionally performed (Dillon 2007; van der Ploeg 1999a). As the threat of military aggression from other states has significantly subsided, security discourses have reframed national security threats in terms of transnational phenomena (Lipschutz 1995; Terriff et al. 1999). In particular, it is the mobility aspect of these phenomena that has become the core security concern. The fact that migration, terrorism, economic flows, electronic crime, and environmental pollution can originate both inside as well as outside a state's territory has significantly diminished the role of state borders in differentiating between internal and external threats. The line between internal and external security has become blurred to the point of fusing the two realms (Bigo 2001).

A key outcome is that security issues are increasingly understood as separated from the institution of the state and more directly connected to everyday life. This change in focus of security concerns has been captured by the concepts of societal security (Buzan 1993; Waever 1993) and human security (de Larrinaga and Doucet 2008; Hyndman 2007). The first suggests that certain transnational phenomena are seen as existential threats to the identity of a social group, while the second refers to the security of the everyday life of the individual. In consequence, there is now a more direct and personal connection between security threats and the individual. Many people feel they experience these threats without the mediation of the state. This perception triggers strong self-defense reactions that can amplify the level of a threat from a personal matter to one of group survival (Lipschutz 1995). Thus the fears people have in their private lives, such as job insecurity or being victims of crime, become more easily projected into the realm of national security (Pickering 2006). Governments have reacted by incorporating these concerns into their security discourses. The Department of Homeland Security, a U.S. security agency created in the wake of September 11, 2001, is representative in this sense. The word *homeland* chosen for this agency has a more personal connotation that evokes the comfort and security of a home, when compared with the word *national*, for example. Homeland security threats speak primarily to Americans as individuals rather than to Americans as a national group.

The result of this shift in the meaning of security has been the penetration of security policies and practices deep into the fabric of society to the level of the individual. It is everyday life rather than state territory that has to be securitized first now in order for the people to be secure (Dillon 2007; Muller 2008). We have moved from securing the national group in order to secure the individual to securing the individual in order to secure the national group. This is a transition from a territorially fixed to a territorially mobile approach to security. The mobilities of everyday life constitute the security risks that have to be controlled now (Lyon 2007a, 2007b). Security strategies now have to be imagined on a global scale, as the trajectories of everyday mobility cannot be easily contained inside state borders (Cresswell 2010; Sheller and Urry 2006).

The implications of this paradigm shift in security are paramount. Seeing everyday life as the object of security strategies increases the relativity of security as a category. One can never go far enough to secure everyday life from all risks. Thus, instead of protecting against explicit threats, security becomes a matter of risk management (Aradau and van Munster 2007; Beck 1998). This is problematic in two ways. First, deciding which of the numerous risks people face in their daily lives constitutes an existential threat to society is an elusive issue. This elusiveness opens up space for the politicization of risk as indicated by the fact that numerous public and private interest groups have joined government elites in the production of national security risks (Amoore 2006, 2009). To this end, some security discourses play down the social risks associated with free trade and environmental pollution while emphasizing risks from migration and organized crime. Others do just the opposite.

Second, risk management is much like predicting the unknown; it takes imagination and speculation rather than fact-based analysis. Risks are in the realm of probabilities. They are about events that have not happened but may potentially happen (Beck 1998). This view encourages the security net to be cast very wide in the society in order to gather a sufficient amount of information to permit identifying patterns of risk that may lead to more explicit security threats. In other words, risks have to be "extracted" from surveillance activities. To accomplish this task effectively, the entire society has to become the object of surveillance activities (Amoore and de Goede 2008; Lyon 2005, 2007a). The working assumption of this logic, that everybody is a potential suspect until one can prove oneself innocent, raises fundamental human rights questions that have not been appropriately addressed so far (Tsoukala 2008).

As a part of the security apparatus, borders play major roles in risk management strategies. They are seen as sites where transnational mobility can be securitized (Ackleson 2005a; Amoore 2006; Hyndman and Mountz 2007). Border securitization is an attempt to render the relativity of risks calculable in order to make them preventable. The expectation is that enhanced border surveillance can lead to risk identification, as the recent convergence between wireless and biometric technologies suggests. In this capacity, borders have emerged as society's security guarantors and have uncritically become part of everyday life.

However, borders are more than risk management sites. They are security constitutive as well. Border-making discourses play active parts in the production of societal and human security risks, for it is at the crossing of a border that someone or something can become a security risk. Othering continues to take center stage in these discourses, with the caveat that the Other has shifted from the neighboring nation to mobile phenomena. Put differently, the blurring of the inside/outside territorial distinction characteristic of modern states has not led to the disappearance of this border-based power practice. Borders continue to provide the basis for inside/outside differentiation with regard to group membership. What has changed is the type of territorial logic involved in Othering, which has moved now beyond fixity to include flexibility and multiplicity, that is, network membership.

Making sense of how security risks come into being and what their relationship to borders is invites a number of questions. Why are some mobility aspects considered existential risks while others are not? Who decides, and on what grounds, which risks to securitize borders against? How do we determine the appropriate amount of resources to allocate to securitizing a risk? How do we know when a risk has been appropriately addressed? These are questions that generally elude clear answers. Yet they are exactly the type of questions that have to be asked when considering border securitization policies with long-ranging consequences for society.

Manipulating Fears to Produce Mobile Risks: Blending Migration, Terrorism, and Crime

Border securitization discourses are dominated by immigration, terrorism, and organized crime. These broad categories can be further broken up into subdivisions. Immigration can be temporary or permanent, skilled or unskilled, legal or illegal, and it can include political refugees fleeing violence in Iraq, Afghanistan, Sudan, Somalia, or Myanmar, as well as immigrants in search of work driven from their lands by poverty in Latin America, sub-Saharan Africa, or South Asia. Terrorism can embrace the mantle of religious fundamentalism as with al-Qaeda or that of political and ethnic separatism as with the Kurdish PKK. There can also be "homegrown" terrorism, as with the 1995 bombing of the Murrah Federal Building in Oklahoma City by Timothy McVeigh. Organized crime can include anything from human to drug to weapon trafficking. Each of these aspects of transnational mobility relates in different ways to borders and calls for individualized security approaches.

In the post-9/11 world, transnational terrorism is widely assumed to be the most important security risk. *Terrorism* is the most widely used word in contemporary border securitization discourses, and it solicits the widest consensus when it comes to border securitization practices. It is commonly assumed that border securitization can keep society safe by preventing terrorists from penetrating state territories. Without doubt, fear of being killed in a terrorist attack unifies people against terrorism risks. However, this fear does not explain either terrorism's position as the most important contemporary threat to the security of a society or the expectation that border securitization translates into effective terrorism prevention. In most societies, car accidents and gun violence kill on a daily basis significantly more people than terrorism does. They are also more random and more preventable than terrorism is. Yet they fail to unify people's actions against them. These facts point to the possibility that the spectacular nature of terrorist acts is being manipulated for political purposes to appear as an existential threat to society.

A closer analysis of current security risks reveals that of all the aspects of transnational mobility, the issues of immigration and organized crime dominated border securitization discourses and practices long before terrorism. Indeed, border securitization policies were long in the making by 2001 (Coleman 2007a, 2007b; Torpey 2000; Walters 2002). Migration in particular still continues to dominate these discourses despite terrorism's higher visibility.

By the early 1990s, immigration had already come to embody trans-national risks in much of Western Europe and the United States (Huys-mans 2006). With the Cold War over and the Soviet Union dismantled, migration offered a tempting new "Other" to rally against. Immigrants became political lighting rods and scapegoats for globalization-induced fears. During the 1990s, East Europeans started to immigrate in sig-nificant numbers to Western Europe, driven by painful economic tran-sitions in their home countries. Refugees from the wars in the former Yugoslavia and the post-Soviet space compounded the issue. Latin Americans and Southeast Asians steadily increased their immigration flows to the United States in search of jobs and opportunity (Nevins 2002). Immigrants become a much more visible presence on the streets of many European cities, as well as in U.S. cities far from the southern borderland. Reports that immigrants were straining local resources available for health care, education, and other public services started to appear in the media. Newspapers reported on Algerian extremists bombing railroad tracks in France, Kurdish activists blowing up Turkish businesses in Germany, and increases in drug traffic–related violence in the United States. Television news media broadcast images showing groups of immigrants swarming over border fences in plain daylight, sneaking across borders at night, or beaching on the Floridian and Medi-terranean shores.

All of these phenomena created the image of an invasion army of immi-grants poised to take over Western societies (van Houtum and Boedeltje 2009; Wonders 2006). State borders appeared broken and incapable of de-fending their societies. Many people in the developed world came to see themselves as being under siege and demanded action from their leaders. Opportunistic politicians sensed an avenue to power by exploiting im-migration fears and embarked on immigrant-Othering discourses. This process deeply politicized immigration and raised its profile. At the least, immigration has been conceived as a new national security risk. That the "invaders" were unarmed and willing to work long hours for little pay in jobs that the developed societies needed to support their lifestyles was of little consequence to the image of the immigrant as a threatening Other. The fact that a significant number of immigrants were refugees in search of asylum did not make much difference either.

For the most part, underneath current immigrant-Othering discourses in developed societies there are fears of a cultural nature. Despite the fact that these discourses are often articulated in economic terms, numerous interest groups embracing them fear less losing their power and privileges to immigrants than they fear immigrants showing up in a house near them. While migration can be a legitimate concern especially at the local scale, there is a long list of other transnational issues that rank ahead in terms of their effects on societal and human security in developed countries. The structure of global economic exchanges, environmental pollution, and political corruption, for example, far outweigh the impact of transnational immigration on most people's lives. Nonetheless, many elected officials and individuals seeking public office, as well as some interest groups, decide that for them it is more politically advantageous to direct popular anger at the least powerful social group rather than take on corporations for outsourcing, address poverty and crime in the inner cities, or increase funding for public services.

Since mid-1980s, several rounds of legislation have been passed in the United States and the European Union to strengthen existing immigration laws (Ackleson 2005a; Coleman 2005, 2007a; Walters 2002). These legislative acts established border securitization as central to the regulation of immigration. Every new round of legislation enhanced border policing capacity, expanded the list of infractions that made immigrants eligible for deportation, and increased investment in border infrastructure (Lahav 2004; Nevins 2002). These measures were typically justified in terms of the need to fight transnational networks of organized crime. They operated with a binary legal-illegal framework that justified the continuation of immigration flows essential to the growth of developed economies while forbidding immigration flows deemed undesirable for economic, cultural, or political reasons.

The problem with the distinction between good versus bad immigrants is twofold. First, it can be argued that everybody crossing a border can be a potential illegal immigrant, as a significant number of immigrants cross state borders legally and then become illegal after they overstay their visas (Torpey 2000). Second, it criminalizes the act of border crossing by making the illegal immigrant guilty of the crime of having crossed a border. In this logic, millions of immigrants in search of jobs or political refuge are associated with criminals. This creates the perception of the immigrant as a societal risk, which in turn encourages the criminalization of immigration as a whole. As a result, immigration legislation tends to ignore differences between various types of immigration, focusing instead on tightening the requirements for legal admission across the board. As more avenues to migrate legally are closed, large immigrant categories such as refugees and temporary migrants increasingly turn to illegal immigration. Illegal immigration continues to grow, and immigration fears in host societies become self-fulfilling security risks.

These two arguments show that border securitization makes a poor solution to immigration control, as it cannot address its root causes. The history and the geography of border securitization forcefully underscore this point. After the erection of border fences in San Diego, California, immigration flows have reoriented toward the deserts of Arizona. Following the same logic, after the erection of border fences around the Spanish enclaves of Ceuta and Melilla in North Africa, African immigration flows to the European Union have shifted out of the West African coast to the Spanish Canary Islands. More mobile solutions such as visas have hardly been more successful. Stricter visa requirements have resulted in increased bribes to the employees of western consulates overseas and have pushed potential legal immigrants to cross illegally. The reality is that the 2007–2011 global recession has done more to curb transnational immigration than all border securitization measures to date.

Early twenty-first-century transnational immigration is largely a result of widening unevenness in global development and of conflict-generated violence. As of 2008, there were an estimated two hundred million transnational immigrants, accounting for approximately 3 percent of the world's population (International Labour Organization 2008). The largest immigration flows are work related (the second largest are refugees) and follow the North-South global divide, from Latin to North America, from Africa to Europe, and from South Asia to the Middle East, Europe, and Australia. In circumstances in which personal mobility becomes a necessity that dictates one's life opportunities in globalization (Bauman 1998; Urry 2000), the pressures for immigration can only be expected to increase. The criminalization of immigration makes this phenomenon even more contentious rather than helping to address it.

After September 11, 2001, the connection between border securitization and transnational mobility has acquired new vigor. Terrorism has provided unprecedented impetus to border securitization by giving it a sense of urgency that the much less exciting issues of immigration and organized crime had difficulty delivering. Terrorism-related fears have been inserted into already-existing immigration and organized crime rhetoric based on the fact that they were all criminal acts perpetrated by mobile outsiders. To this end, many post-9/11 border security discourses mention terrorism, immigration, and organized crime in the same sentence. Lumping these vastly different phenomena together has erased the distinctions between them and led to a one-size-fits-all border securitization approach (Ackleson 2005a; Walters 2002). Across the world, terrorists caught crossing borders are few and far between. Many terrorist acts, such as the ones in Madrid in 2004 and in London in 2005, have been perpetrated by insiders or by people residing legally in those countries. Lacking captured terrorists, border securitization measures justified in the name of fighting terrorism end up being used to control immigration.

Networking and Privatizing Border Making

Border securitization discourses and practices have led to a double transformation in the nature of borders. Striving to achieve selective permeability, numerous aspects of border management have been externalized and internalized as well as privatized (Lahav and Guiraudon 2000; Rumford 2007). The first aspect has to do with the spatiality of borders and involves the performance of border functions at a distance from state border lines proper (Coleman 2007a, 2007b; Hyndman and Mountz 2008; Rumford 2006a). At the core of the externalization and internalization of border control is the realization that immigration, terrorism, and organized crime cannot be successfully addressed at state border lines. The response from government stakeholders and from numerous private interest groups has been to expand border securitization practices to deal with these issues before they reach state borders as well as inside state borders. Thus the possibility that border reinforcement does not stop unwanted mobility because it cannot address its root causes has been dismissed. Instead, the position that border reinforcement does not stop unwanted mobility because we have not been good enough at it has been widely adopted. Accordingly, governments at the receiving end of these phenomena have embarked on a strategy to externalize and localize their regulation.

The second aspect—privatization—refers to the issue of authority over borders and involves changes in the nature of the actors engaged in border making as well as their multiplication (Rumford 2008b; Sparke 2004; Vaughan-Williams 2008). Central here are accountability implications emerging from the participation of private actors in border making. In their capacity as territorial limits of the public institution of the state, borders are situated in the public domain. Modern state borders have been historically regulated through public institutions. More recently, governments embracing the logic of neoliberalism have delegated certain border management responsibilities to an array of private groups and quasi-public institutions, and even to private citizens. At the same time, other private interest groups have inserted themselves into the border-making business without the encouragement of governments. The result has been a blurring of the lines between private and public border-making actors that makes it more difficult to establish where accountability for border management lies. Generally, these developments signal the waning of democratic control over borders. While the point has been made that many of the new actors act on behalf of the state (Torpey 2000), there is substantial evidence that they have grown to be much more than simple tools of the state (Rumford 2008b). Sharing border management responsibilities or mobilizing sizeable segments of civil society to take public stances on border issues offers efficient avenues for influencing aspects of border policy making. The problem is not with the increased number of border-making actors; rather it is with the ambiguous legal status regarding their border-making roles.

The changing nature and structure of state borders has resulted in a complex and networked geography of bordering practices. Several such practices with regard to terrorism and organized crime were previously discussed in chapters 3 and 4. They include terrorist detention camps, rendition, and the regulation of offshore financial centers. Additional border management practices preponderantly oriented toward immigration control complete this picture.

Border Internalization and Privatization

Domestically, central governments pursuing neoliberal strategies are increasingly devolving immigration management responsibilities to local authorities and private actors. In the United States, where immigration enforcement has normally been reserved for federal authorities, local police departments have been routinely subcontracted to enforce immigration law (Coleman 2007a, 2007b). In addition, after 2005, U.S. borders have been expanded one hundred miles inward for law enforcement purposes (Davidson and Kim 2009). Within this area, Border Patrol officers have been granted the power to stop vehicles and question passengers regarding their immigration status without probable cause. Such powers represent a rare exception from the protections offered by the Fourth Amendment to the U.S. Constitution that require law enforcement to demonstrate probable cause and obtain a warrant before stopping or searching a person. Traditionally these exceptions were restricted to law enforcement officers stationed at official border-crossing checkpoints. The full implications of the one-hundred-mile-wide law enforcement borderland emerge only when we realize that this includes approximately two-thirds of the U.S. population, or 197 million people based on 2007 U.S. Census data. The largest U.S. cities, from Boston to New York, and from Seattle to Los Angeles, as well as entire states such as Florida, Massachusetts, Hawaii, and others all fall within this expanded borderland.

Throughout the developed world, governments have enacted employer sanctions intended to prevent businesses from employing illegal immigrants. Accordingly, employers are required to perform border work and check their employees' immigration status. In addition, some

governments require landlords to register foreign nationals with the local authorities, while hotel managers and travel agents are required to
document their customers' immigration status (Lahav and Guiraudon
2000). Universities in the United States are also required to report the
enrollment status of foreign students to the immigration authorities
every semester. In other instances, security firms and private contrac-
tors are contracted to run immigrant detention prisons, perform border
security checks, build border fences, and supply sophisticated border
control technologies. Lately, border securitization has expanded to
include cyberspace as well. In numerous countries, Internet café users
are required to register their identity, while in the United States, border
enforcement authorities have required online travel agencies such as
Orbitz and Expedia to update their sites to collect more detailed traveler
information.

In the wake of the terrorist attacks in New York in 2001 and London
in 2005, public advertising campaigns are asking citizens to engage in
detective work and inform authorities of fellow citizens' suspicious behavior and activities (Vaughan-Williams 2008). In other instances, civil
society groups have put borders at the center of their social agendas.
Social movements using slogans such as "No Borders" and "No One Is
Illegal" advocate the abolition of border controls and the free movement
of people, while border-watch groups like the "Minutemen" in the United
States want to restrict movement across borders (Rumford 2008b). In Italy
the government has allowed volunteer citizen groups to patrol the streets
of Italian cities to alert the police to the presence of potential illegal immigrants or criminal behavior.

Border Externalization and Privatization

Carrier sanctions are among the earliest manifestations of border externalization and privatization. They are aimed at immigrants who attempt to
cross borders without appropriate travel documents using various means
of transportation such as airlines, trailer trucks, cargo ships, and trains.
If caught at the border, they become the responsibility of the receiving
state. The idea behind carrier sanctions is to fine transport companies that
bring passengers (knowingly or not) without proper travel documents to
the destination country. This policy has forwarded the responsibility of
passport and visa control to the employees of the companies in the countries where the travel originates, thus well before passengers arrive at the
formal borders of the destination country (Walters 2006b). These practices
leave no legal alternative for people who have to flee conflict situations
or for whom proper documentation is out of the question. They would
have to travel illegally at greater risks. In Somalia, for example, there is

no foreign consulate to issue a visa, and often not even a state institution to issue a passport.

More recent border securitization practices have continued to employ spatial strategies to restrict access to the territories of developed countries (Hyndman and Mountz 2007). Numerous developed countries deploy immigration liaison officers to large airports and ports abroad to work with the local authorities there to help prevent potential illegal immigrants from embarking. Protected entry procedures recently adopted by the European Union encourage potential refugees to apply for asylum at embassies abroad rather than risking the trip all the way to the borders of the European Union. Advanced border patrols at sea frequently operate illegally in international waters to intercept potential immigrants before they reach the shore. They can include a combination of vessels, sophisticated radar systems, planes, and helicopters. The U.S. Coast Guard has patrolled Caribbean waters since the 1980s. The Australian Navy is patrolling the waters near Indonesia and Papua New Guinea, while Italian and Spanish vessels patrol in the Mediterranean and along the West African coast. More recently, border securitization has even gone supranational. In 2004, the European Union established Frontex, an agency in charge of integrating the management of its external borders (Vaughan-Williams 2008). Joint European-Libyan teams have patrolled inside Libyan territorial waters, while joint European-Mauritanian teams have patrolled the Mauritanian coastline by water and air.

The networking of borders is not limited to these practices. It has become incorporated into standard government policy in many developed countries, from where it has been exported to the rest of the world. Initially, border securitization practices have been confined to developed countries. While a great deal of immigration takes place among developing countries, the vast majority of developing-world governments have more pressing priorities to address. By the 2000s, however, this situation changed, and border securitization practices have been globalized. Developed countries have incorporated immigration concerns into their foreign relations with sending and transit countries, typically by making favorable visa policies, development aid, and other assistance conditional on commitment to border securitization.

During the 1990s, the European Union demanded that candidate countries in Eastern Europe like Poland and Romania securitize their eastern borders with neighbors like Ukraine and Moldova. This policy included the introduction of visa regimes and the implementation of state-of-the-art border control technologies. In addition to cofinancing these projects, the European Union has conditioned the compliance of East European governments with their citizens' visa-free access to the EU space. In this way, the EU borders with respect to immigration, organized crime, and a number of economic matters expanded to Eastern Europe years before the countries in the region become EU members (Popescu 2008). Today, the European Union continues these practices through the European Neighborhood Policy (ENP) aimed at enhancing cooperation with its new neighbors. The ENP agreements have helped to expand certain regulatory aspects of the European Union's border even farther eastward and southward to sixteen countries in Eastern Europe, South Caucasus, the Middle East, and North Africa. The United States has followed similar practices in the context of NAFTA, encouraging Mexico to reinforce its southern borders with Guatemala in order to relax border procedures at the common border in the north (Coleman 2007a).

Readmission and safe third-country agreements are other widely employed foreign policy practices. They allow destination countries to repatriate illegal immigrants to their country of origin and to turn back refugees to file asylum claims in the last country they traversed prior to their arrival at their intended destination (Hyndman and Mountz 2007). These practices have opened the doors to the establishment of offshore refugee detention and processing centers inside the borders of third countries (see figure 5.1). Immigrants intercepted trying to enter the European Union, the United States, or Australia are often treated like common criminals and returned to countries as diverse as Ukraine, Turkey, Libya, Mauritania, Guatemala, or Nauru without assessing their asylum claims. This practice is called *refoulement* and is prohibited in the Geneva Refugee Convention as well as in the constitutions of the European countries themselves. Some of the third countries where the immigrants are *refouled* have questionable human rights records and no adequate economic means to support the refugees. The immigrants are imprisoned in abuse-ridden detention camps for months or even years until their cases are processed. Most are deported back to their countries of origin by the third country's authorities, often without proper assessment of their asylum claims.

The offshore immigrant detention camp system is complemented by an interior one where refugees that have already crossed developed-state borders are detained. The United States imprisons about 400,000 immigrants (including children) per year in 350 county jails and private prisons at an annual cost of $2.4 billion (Bernstein 2009). The majority of detainees have no criminal record. In the European Union, in 2008 there were about 224 immigrant detention centers that hosted over 30,000 detainees (Brothers 2008).

A third kind of immigrant detention camp, generally located on isolated islands and in other remote places with ambiguous sovereignty status, deserves special attention. Such examples are Guantanamo (used as a U.S. immigrant detention camp for Cubans and Haitians during the 1980s

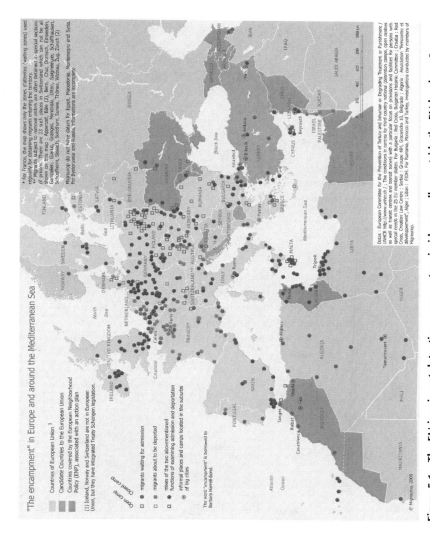

Figure 5.1 The EU immigrant detention camp system inside as well as outside the EU borders. *Source:* Migreurop.

and 1990s before it was converted to a terrorist detention camp during the 2000s), Guam, Christmas Island, and others (Mountz 2011). Detainees are kept hidden from public scrutiny, and in certain cases they have been denied access to basic rights such as immigration lawyers or medical assistance. This strategy is part of a larger trend of manipulating state borders to include some territories for some purposes while excluding them for other purposes. In-between places are created that are situated inside and outside national borders at the same time. Their purpose is to allow states to avoid sovereignty responsibilities at their own will.

The immigration policy adopted by the Australian government in 2001 best illustrates these border-making practices (Green 2006; Hyndman and Mountz 2008). Asian immigrants intercepted at sea have been denied landing on the Australian mainland and were instead diverted thousands of kilometers away to detention camps on the Australian-held Cocos and Christmas islands in the Indian Ocean. Others have been diverted to islands in the Pacific Ocean belonging to independent states such as Nauru, Papua New Guinea, and Indonesia that have been paid by the Australian government to accept the refugees. Another aspect of the plan has consisted in the exclusion of several thousand islands from the Australian territory for immigration purposes (Hyndman and Mountz 2008). Immigrants landing on these islands were not considered to be on Australian soil and were not allowed to file asylum claims in Australia. What is more, some islands were excluded retroactively, after the immigrants had arrived there. Under these circumstances, the Australian borders had become the ultimate expression of mobility, to the point of leaving the real and entering the metaphysical. In a mystifying exercise of spatial and temporal acrobatics, these borders were bending and stretching around the bodies of the immigrants without ever touching them. On display here was the raw power of border making. This policy came to an end in 2008 when a new government came to power in Australia. However, the practice of detaining immigrants on the remote Christmas Island continues (see figure 5.2).

Bearing the Hidden and the Not-So-Hidden Costs

The border securitization regime has led to the creation of a global archipelago of immigrant detention camps that closely mirrors the terrorist detention camps discussed in chapter 3. These archipelagos defy established understandings of foreign and domestic as well as public and private. They are situated in part inside state borders, in part outside them, and in part in between. Also, they are in part public and in part private. They occupy political-territorial interstitial spaces for which we have only recently started to develop a language to allow us to make sense of them.

Figure 5.2   Australian immigrant detention center on Christmas Island. *Source:* Australian Department of Immigration and Citizenship.

Little-heard-of places such as Lampedusa (Italy), Kufrah (Libya), Sangatte (France), Christmas Island (Australia), T. don Hutto (the United States), Guantanamo (Cuba), Diego Garcia (the UK), and Lindela (South Africa), together with hundreds of other such places, have come to embody the drama of the twenty-first-century security paradigm.

Much of this drama has ended in death (van Houtum and Boedeltje 2009). Thousands have perished from thirst or exhaustion in the deserts of the U.S.-Mexico borderland. Thousands more have drowned before reaching Europe's shores. Their bodies have occasionally washed up on Mediterranean beaches among European beachgoers. Others die asphyxiated in truck trailers while being smuggled across borders, or they are crushed under tires when they fail to climb inside the trailer of a moving truck. And then there are the ones, nobody knows how many, who die without anyone knowing they died. What puts these deaths into perspective is that they happened while trying to avoid being caught crossing the border to a better life, not to invade a country.

The direct economic costs of border securitization for developed countries are enormous. Border making in the twenty-first century is a worldwide multi-billion-dollar business that in addition to governments involves a variety of industries, from construction companies, to airlines, to hardware and software developers, to security firms, to financial corporations, to name only a selected few beneficiaries. These hundreds of billions of dollars are public money invested in border security at a time of massive spending cuts in public education, health care, and other social programs. Such logic begs several questions: What are the benefits of these investments for society? Is the wealth created by public investments in border security worth the losses created by public disinvestment in social programs when it comes to the well-being of societies? Can these billions bring better security returns if strategically invested in the sending societies?

The work of the Italian philosopher Giorgio Agamben (1998, 2005) on the interactions between sovereignty, power strategies, and human life offers a valuable path for interpreting the more insidious effects current border-making practices are having on society. Agamben has shown how sovereignty can allow states to manipulate their laws to produce a paradoxical "state of exception" in which people are legally stripped of the protections offered by the juridical system while remaining legally under the control of the state, thus exposed to the abuses of its powers (Gregory 2007). He points to prison camps—from Nazi concentration camps, to Guantanamo, to immigrant detention camps—as archetypical "spaces of exception" where human beings exist in a state of in-betweenness, at once outside and inside the bounds of the law. From the perspective of border studies, securitization practices manipulate borders to create spaces of exception—situated outside and inside state borders at once—where mobility can be isolated and regulated in extrajuridical terms. In these spaces, humans cease to be seen as subjects of state power that bear political rights. They are reduced to their condition as biological life-forms, mere bodies that are alive.

Agamben (2005) also warns against seeing these "spaces of exception" as a matter of external concern that affects only outsiders. When exceptional powers are repeatedly used, they tend to become established as a mode of governance that infuses everyday life. The rare exception becomes the ubiquitous norm. Then extrajuridical state power escapes the space of the camp and turns inward to oppress the society in the name of protecting it. Put differently, the geography of the "spaces of exception" should not be narrowly understood only in terms of clearly identifiable territories situated in remote places. Rather, the "spaces of exception" are a political-geographical condition that inhabits multiple locales in society. The point most often missed about border securitization practices is that they change the very societies they claim to protect by eroding the political rights available to their own members, therefore leaving them more insecure and exposed to the whims of power. In a world where the lines between outside and inside and between public and private are blurred, eschewing legal responsibilities through practices such as interception in international waters, repatriation of immigrants to unsafe places, rendition, indefinite detention, and others, outsiders and insiders alike end up being affected.

EMBODYING BORDERS:
TECHNO-CONQUERING THE ULTIMATE FRONTIER

Risk-based border securitization practices have brought the human body into the spotlight. If borders are about achieving power through the ordering of difference in space, then the dispersion of border-making strategies to the smallest and most personal of spaces—the body—appears natural. In this logic, bodies are imagined as spaces to inscribe borders on. They become border bodyscapes.

Embodied borders present obvious advantages. They are highly mobile and utterly individual, allowing constant and accurate movement control at the smallest spatial scale. From this perspective, they are seen by many as the breakthrough that settles globalization's security versus mobility bordering dilemma. Mobile risks can be estimated from mobile bodies and efficiently eliminated at the border so that traffic flows are not disrupted. The body makes the ideal border, as it is always at hand, ready to be performed whenever circumstances require. Given such attributes, the appeal of embodied borders is immense. It is the promise of unmitigated power over the movements of the human being that largely explains why policy makers and corporations around the world have enthusiastically embraced embodied borders.

The body has long been a subject of bordering practices (Tyner 2006). The health checks for immigrants at Ellis Island over a century ago, where unable bodies were denied access to the New World, are just one such example. Nonetheless, until the early twenty-first century the body has eluded unmitigated control. It has remained a loosely governed frontier space, trespassed by many power practices but also populated by numerous resistance movements. Today, the body is at once the subject of bordering practices and their bordering agent. The border has been embedded in the body (Sassen 2006). We have thus reached a point where the body has become itself the border. The individual is a walking, talking border.

Identity plays a key role in the process of embodying borders. The underlying assumption is that a person's identity makes a good risk predictor. Therefore, the identity of the individual provides the basis for identifying the risk it poses to society. All that remains to be done to secure space and society is to find an efficient way to check people's identities at all times when they move through borders. To solve this problem, policy makers and business groups have increasingly put their faith in monitoring technology. Over the last decade, digital information technology has provided the vital medium for articulating the body-border-identity connection. The outcome has been the emergence of a vast array of sophisticated technologies—many with origins in military applications—that are used to embed borders into bodies in order to detect them, identify them, and track their movements. They include heartbeat and CO_2 emission detectors, heat radars, wireless communication systems, and others. Among these, biometrics and radio frequency identification (RFID) technologies stand out because of their transformative impacts on society's relationship with space. Suggestively, U.S. and Canadian officials have dubbed this technology-driven border regime "Smart Borders" (Ackleson 2005b; Sparke 2004).

Biometric Bordering and the Production of Identity

Biometric borders are primarily geared to tackle the security aspect of globalization's bordering dilemma. Biometrics are measurements of a person's unique physiological characteristics to verify or establish their identity. They can be derived from reading diverse body parts such as facial geometry, fingerprints, or iris patterns, as well as from behavioral traits such as voice, signature, and keystroke (Epstein 2008; Lodge 2007). Early biometrics used in predigital passports usually included pictures, signatures, eye color, and height (Salter 2003). Modern biometric technologies use digital sensor devices (e.g., cameras and scanners) to automatically acquire bodily data that are then algorithmically encrypted and stored for retrieval in centralized databases and on chips inserted into personal documents such as passports and visas (van der Ploeg 1999b). At a border-crossing point, a person has to present the body part together with the e-travel document in order to be identified. The person's identity will then be digitally read from his or her body and checked against the data stored in databases or on chips. If a match is found, this verifies their identity (see figure 5.3).

Modern biometric technologies were initially used on a small scale during the 1990s, mainly in banking to grant secure access to money and in security establishments to control access to buildings and other spaces. During the early 2000s they were incorporated into border securitization practices in the United States and Europe to control illegal immigration and to manage trusted traveler schemes (Sparke 2006; van der Ploeg 1999a). By the late 2000s, biometrics had become mainstays of border securitization regimes from Thailand and Australia to Nigeria and the United States. They are being used in large-scale applications affecting hundreds of millions of people, most notably through government-issued biometric passports (also known as e-passports) (see figure 5.4) and through the setup of numerous border-related databases. Underlining their appeal is

Figure 5.3 Biometric measurement at the border. *Source:* **U.S. Customs and Border Patrol.**

the assumption of infallible personal identification as summarized by the expression "the body does not lie" (Aas 2006). The belief is that the more accurately bodily characteristics can be technologically captured and interpreted, the more human subjectivity can be eliminated from the system and the more unfaltering personal identification becomes.

Despite the use of biometrics in bordering practices before September 11, 2001, there is little doubt that the attacks on New York and Washington, D.C., provided critical impetus for their wide-scale adoption. First officially heralded by the U.S. Patriot Act of 2001, biometric technologies became generalized with the U.S. Enhanced Border Security and Visa Entry Reform Act of 2002, which mandated the creation of interoperational biometric immigration databases, as well as the introduction of U.S. biometric travel documents. One particular provision of this law stipulated that the Visa Waiver countries, whose citizens could visit the United States without a visa for up to three months, would have to introduce biometric e-passports as well if they wished to maintain these privileges. These legal provisions reaching outside the borders of the United States effectively worked to globalize the border securitization regime based on biometrics. The process was bolstered in 2003 when the International Civil Aviation Organization, a UN body comprising 190 states that regulates air traffic, recommend the adoption of biometric e-passports

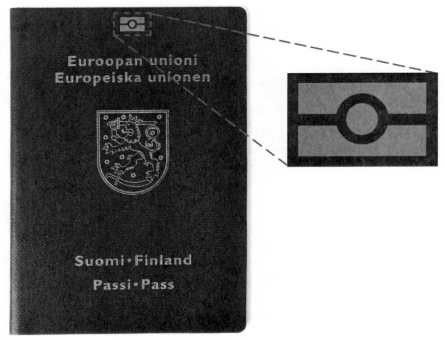

Figure 5.4   Biometric passport. *Source:* **The Finnish Border Guard.**

including digitized photographs as the new standard for international travel documents. The governments of the European Union were initially outraged by U.S. demands. Soon thereafter, citing their own border securitization reasons, they decided to introduce biometric e-passports based not on one but two sets of biometrics, photos and fingerprints (Epstein 2007). This situation has left many governments in the developing world little choice but to follow suit, investing in biometric technologies in order to meet the passport standards demanded by developed countries.

The rapid diffusion of biometric technologies as a panacea for border securitization owes a great deal to the conflation of identification with identity. This means that identifying a person's body is the same as knowing a person's identity. Accordingly, biometric identification is used in two major ways: to verify someone's identity and to establish someone's identity (Lyon 2008; van der Ploeg 1999b). The first use is most commonly associated with current e-travel documents. In this instance, the use of biometrics is predicated upon the need to verify a person's identity to confirm that they are who they say they are. The body works much like a password, providing personal identification on the move to gain access to diverse spaces and services. From this vantage point, biometric passports and IDs are simply updated versions of previous identification documents. They are quicker, more efficient, and more precise than their predecessors. They are also believed to be virtually tamper proof.

However, just as the value of biometrics for border securitization appears to be self-evident, it is also the case that biometric passports would not be able to stop potential terrorists at the U.S. border just like nondigital passports did not stop them before September 11, 2001 (Salter 2004). The point is that verifying Osama bin Laden's identity, even biometrically, would only have confirmed that he was who he said he was. Biometrics stored on bin Laden's passport chip would not have said that he was a terrorist. For that to happen, security systems would need to possess previous information regarding the actions of the person identified as Osama bin Laden that could be linked in some way to the biometrics in his passport chip.

There is a second use of biometrics aimed at addressing the question, "Who is this person?" Answering this question requires establishing a person's identity. In this case, biometric systems have to perform sophisticated investigative work to identify one person from a group of people. They have to compare someone's biometrics to those of a multitude of other individuals. This task necessitates the establishment and maintenance of databases to store biometrics from a large number of people. Biometric passports and IDs that a person can carry with them have to be linked to databases that are administered separately by the border-crossing authorities of each country or by each security company and are stored locally in intranet networks. Ideally, for biometric technologies to work best, there should be one global database that contains several types of biometrics for each person, enrolls the entire population of the planet, and is stored in cyberspace to be easily accessible.

Nonetheless, vast volumes of biometric data alone are still not sufficient to meaningfully determine someone's identity (van der Ploeg 1999b). For this, databases have to contain additional information about peoples' everyday lives that can be electronically mined to reveal patterns of behavior and association. Once someone's biometrics are recorded into a database, personal information can be collected every time there is a hit on them. In other words, every time someone's identity is checked biometrically, this leaves a trace in a database that is stored under that person's profile according to predetermined criteria such as name, address, country of origin, how many times somebody crosses a border, which borders were crossed and in what places, means of transportation used, form of payment for the trip, duration of stay, driving history, type of meal consumed in flight, seating preference, and more (Department of Homeland Security 2006). This is how a person's digital identity takes shape in a database without the person even being aware of it. The belief is that these border security systems will prevent the repetition of situations like September 11, 2001, by allowing law enforcement authorities to "connect the dots" between apparently unrelated bits of information. Such systems have been functioning in secret at U.S. borders since 2002 (they have been declassified in 2006) under the name of Automated Targeting Systems (ATS). They integrate several separate governmental and private databases and have collected data on hundreds of millions of U.S. visitors and U.S. citizens alike. In addition, there is also a parallel ATS system that assigns risk scores to all goods crossing U.S. borders. The European Union is implementing similar systems dubbed Automated Border Control (ABC) (Guild et al. 2008).

When this entire infrastructure is in place at the border-crossing points, computerized software reads the passport chip and the body part, identifies personal data in the database, and then analyzes them according to a secret algorithm that produces a person's identity profile with a calculated risk score assigned to it (Amoore 2009). Technically, this makes border guards redundant (see figure 5.5). The end product is a computer-generated identity that few understand but that everybody has to trust. This is what the computer at the automated border gate says: "Sir/Madam, here is who you are. I read it from your palm, your finger, and your iris. You need not utter a word. This will only increase your processing time and create congestion. I am confident I know who you

Figure 5.5   Automated border gates at Helsinki International Airport. Source: The Finnish Border Guard.

ought to be. You may go on with your day now/You may step out of line for additional screening now."

Two main types of biometric databases are at the core of the Smart Borders concept. The first is designed to assist catching the unwanted. These are the databases that contain all biometrics collected from travelers at border-crossing points, when they apply for visas, or when they acquire biometric passports and IDs. This category also includes so-called terrorist watch lists, no-fly lists, and databases of asylum seekers and criminal offenders. This is the most widespread type of biometric database. It enrolls the most people and stores the most private information about them. From a risk management perspective, these databases are pools of suspects from which the risky bodies can be identified. They are managed through a series of programs among which the largest to date is the $10 billion US-VISIT program collecting the biometrics of all foreign citizens entering the United States (Amoore 2006; Epstein 2008). ATS-type programs also fit in this category. In the European Union, three such programs stand out: Eurodac, used for immigration purposes and containing the fingerprints of asylum claimants; the Schengen Information System (SIS), used for immigration and crime-related purposes, primarily to identify wanted third-country nationals to be denied entry into the European Union; and the Visa Information System (VIS), used for immigration and law enforcement purposes, collecting data on all third-country nationals who need visas to enter the European Union (Baldaccini 2008). Japan, Australia, and Brazil, together with several other countries, also have biometric data collection programs, albeit of a more modest scale.

The second type of biometric database is designed to enhance mobility and is most commonly associated with registered traveler programs operating at various border-crossing checkpoints from Hong Kong and Indonesia to Portugal and the United States. Many such programs are public-private partnerships, underwritten by state security agencies and implemented by private security firms. Well-known registered traveler schemes are Privium, operating at Amsterdam's Schiphol Airport; SmartGate, in operation at several Australian airports; and Global Entry, operating at large U.S. airports. Among the largest are NEXUS between the United States and Canada, and SENTRI (Secure Electronic Network for Travelers Rapid Inspection) between the United States and Mexico (Sparke 2006). There is also a prescreening infrastructure for cross-border trade that parallels the one for people. One of the largest such programs is FAST (Fast and Secure Trade), between the United States, Canada, and Mexico. The idea behind these programs is to determine people's identities ahead of time in order to grant them the privilege of experiencing the borderless world while at the same time reducing the economic costs of border securitization. For a fee, people can obtain security clearance by undergoing a priori security checks that include collection of their biometrics. This assigns them "low-risk" or "trusted" traveler status, which in turn grants them preferential border-crossing treatment such as access to automated border control gates at airports or to dedicated traffic lanes at land borders. In essence, this is self-service border crossing that promises to reduce border-crossing time to seconds and to avoid cumbersome security procedures. The Iris Recognition Immigration System (IRIS) program available at several UK airports goes one step further and does away with any form of document control. Having their biometrics already stored in the database, IRIS customers need only present their body part (in this case the iris) for identification upon their arrival at the automatic border control gate (UK Border Agency 2010).

The Age of Remote Control: RFIDing Mobilities

RFID borders are primarily geared for tackling the mobility aspect of globalization's bordering dilemma. RFID is a generic term that refers to electronic systems capable of transmitting information containing the identity of an object or person wirelessly using radio waves (Juels 2006). An RFID device, called a tag, consists of a microchip storing identifiable information in the form of a unique numeric code and a miniature antenna that when activated transmits and receives information to and from a computerized reading system. RFID readers can identify a large number of tags present at the same time in the same place. The tags' reading range varies from up to thirty feet for passive tags that lack their own power source, to up to three hundred feet for active tags that have their own power source. The former are the smallest, cheapest, and the most widespread. When in the vicinity of an RFID reading system, they receive a radio signal that activates them to broadcast the information stored on the chip.

The appeal of RFID technology lies in the possibility of automated remote control identification while on the move, which reduces transaction costs and speeds up flows by minimizing human intervention. In essence, this amounts to a high-tech surveillance tool that enables tracking the location of objects and people in a network at any time without stopping them (Amoore 2009; Dobson and Fisher 2007). Originating in military applications developed during World War II, RFID technology was adopted on a large scale for commercial purposes during the 1990s to track in real time the location of inventory in global supply chains such as Walmart. Today, RFID tags are poised to replace bar codes on products. A majority of globally traded goods are identified through RFID tags. The technology is also widely used in automated toll payment systems. Moreover, RIFD tags the size of a grain of rice have even been implanted in human bodies to help track people in case of kidnapping, to grant them access to secure areas, or for medical purposes (Albrecht 2008; Juels 2006).

After 2005, RFID technology made it into mainstream bordering practices, where it has been married with biometrics. RFID tags are used as a means for wirelessly transmitting personal information and biometrics stored in the chips embedded in e-travel documents (see figure 5.6). The tags broadcast a uniquely encrypted code that allows a computer system access to personal biometrics from an e-passport microchip or from a database (Hoepman et al. 2006; Koscher et al. 2009). Using RFID readers, the data from a passport together with the assigned security risk score from the ATS database can already be displayed on the border guard's computer screen by the time a person arrives at the kiosk (Department of Homeland Security 2008). Furthermore, in the case of automated border gates and preferred traveler schemes, RFID technology promises to make the borderless world come true for those deemed "low risk" (Amoore 2009). They can be identified and assessed while casually moving through borders.

At the outset of the 2010s, RFID technology is becoming standard in travel documents, rapidly replacing optical machine-readable passports, visas, residence permits, and other IDs that require manual swiping. U.S. passports have included RFID technology since 2006. Over sixty other countries are issuing RFID-encrypted passports as well. Nonetheless,

Figure 5.6 RFID-enabled checkpoint at the U.S.-Canada border. *Source:* U.S. Customs and Border Patrol.

international interoperability remains to be achieved for the system to work on a global scale. Without interoperability, RFID technology is of limited use in bordering practices, as the biometrics stored in e-passports issued in one country cannot be accessed wirelessly by border guards in other countries. Integrating passport RFID technology means that essential technical information, such as access codes, de-encryption algorithms, and databases, has to be shared across borders to allow quick access to a person's biometric identity. Sharing this information implies that identifiable biometric information and the means to interpret it will have to be available for worldwide access by a multitude of people and agencies.

The Not-So-Smart "Smart Borders"

A critical examination of the assumptions intrinsic to the Smart Borders regime casts major doubts over its logic of reconciling mobility and security via risk-based identity management. The gap between the expectations for this border regime and what it is actually able to deliver is simply too wide. Far from being "smart," the regime can be quite dumb in some respects and even potentially dangerous in others. The costs in financial terms and, more important, from the point of view of democratic life far outweigh the security benefits such a border regime can bring to society. To be sure, bordering practices and innovative technologies can play a role in securing twenty-first-century mobility. The problem is with the prominent roles assigned to border technologies in security strategies and with the resulting power shifts in society (Amoore 2009; Salter 2004).

The implementation of the Smart Borders regime raises two broad sets of technical concerns related to security and privacy issues. Chief among the fallacies of the Smart Borders logic is its overreliance on technology. This reliance promotes a view of security as simply a technical problem that requires a technical fix, and assumes that the world's structural problems can be addressed by bordering them away with the help of technology. These beliefs have become so entrenched that even when the border security apparatus faces systemic failures, the answer is to introduce more sophisticated technologies to expand surveillance practices rather than to question the overall utility of the system. The Christmas Day 2009 airplane bombing attempt over Detroit is of particular relevance in this respect because it happened *after* all border security systems discussed earlier were in place (Sullivan 2009). The successful attempt by a young Nigerian national, radicalized in the UK and with ties to al-Qaeda in Yemen, to smuggle and ignite explosives hidden in his underwear on a U.S.-bound plane points to more than a failure of border security technologies to detect explosives or to a failure of intelligence agencies to connect the dots in their vast databases.

This incident challenged the very logic behind a border security regime in which worldwide mass surveillance practices are justified in terms of necessary evils to secure social life. Risk scores, biometric data, and other information on hundreds of millions of bodies have been worthless in preventing the underwear bomber from crossing borders. This fact suggests that a smaller, nimbler, and more targeted system, reliant on specific human intelligence, could have better chances of providing more effective security. Ultimately, the reality is that when the U.S. database of terrorism suspects alone contains over half a million people, the United States has more than a border securitization problem.

Particularly questionable is the assumption that biometrics and RFID make identity management technologies infallible. This reflects a strain of Cartesianism-informed technological determinism that is blind to the fact that the social use of technology is a two-way street. Technology alone cannot provide exclusive benefits to security agencies and law-abiding citizens. A society evolves with its technology, including peoples' capacity to defeat the system. For example, e-passports have been proved surprisingly vulnerable to hacking via their RFID capabilities. Commercially available RFID tag readers have been used by researchers to break the encryption codes stored in e-passport chips and to copy their contents (Albrecht 2008). This means that biometric and other personal data can be remotely stolen from e-passports through someone's purse or pocket without the owner's knowledge. The data can then be cloned into a new e-passport chip to impersonate the owner at a border-crossing checkpoint (Koscher et al. 2009). Other RFID shortcomings include the possibility of eavesdropping on communication between a chip and a reader, the "killing" of a chip by sending a signal that disables it, the tracking of people remotely, and the identification of peoples' citizenship to use it, for example, to explode a bomb when a citizen of a specific country passes by (Hoepman et al. 2006).

These issues are addressed by continuously upgrading RFID security features in e-travel documents to close all foreseeable loopholes (Liersch 2009). However, this cannot address the core problem that remote control bordering raises because its nature is not technological. All that e-passport RFID technology can do at its best is to faithfully transmit bits of information from the chips to a reading system that confirms that the data from the chip are authentic. What this technology cannot do is tell whether the person holding the passport is the same as the owner of the data from the chip. Human intervention, in the form of inspections by vigilant border guards who make sure the biometrics on the computer screen match the ones of the person at the border checkpoint, remains the most reliable technique to detect forged e-passports. What, then, are the benefits of this technology from the perspective of societal and human security? Is it really making people more secure? Who is benefiting the most from its incorporation into border practices?

In their turn, biometrics have their own shortcomings (Lodge 2007). They cannot offer 100 percent identification accuracy in all cases. Rather, they offer a high statistical probability of a positive match between a body part and a previously submitted sample of the body part. For example, certain categories of people like the elderly, Asian women, the disabled, and others present physical features that are difficult to enroll in biometric programs like fingerprinting. Biometric systems at the border flag members of such groups more often, thus discriminating against them. Moreover, fingerprint readers have been successfully fooled at the border by attaching silicon patches to a person's fingertips, as well as by surgically grafting patches of skin from other parts of the body to the fingertips (Heussner 2009). Face and iris recognition systems can be deceived as well. The answer to these issues has been to demand the use of even more biometrics. The next generation of e-passports will include two or more biometrics to minimize the chance of fraud. Even better, the latest biometric systems can determine whether the body part to be identified belongs to a live body or not.

Additional concerns involve the securing of immense biometric databases that would have to be accessed in thousands of locations worldwide. If they are lost, corrupted, or hacked into, the damage to the lives of people affected can be incalculable. What is important to realize about this kind of personal data is that once they are lost, the victims would bear the consequences for the rest of their lives. Since these are bodily data, one cannot just declare them lost and have new ones issued.

In effect, biometric borders push the issue of security further inside society instead of resolving it. The fact that peoples' biometrics have to be prerecorded in travel documents and databases in order for biometric systems at the border to work means that biometric borders can be only as secure as the process of biometric enrollment. Instead of physically tampering with an e-passport or with somebody's fingertips, it becomes more effective to forge the much less sophisticated feeder documents required to establish a biometric identity, such as birth certificates, proof of residence, and other documents. In this way, a known terrorist or a spy can acquire a perfectly authentic biometric identity under another name at a passport-issuing office somewhere in the world. Provided that biometric border databases do not contain the terrorist's or spy's recent photograph, fingerprints, or iris scans—and all indications are that in many cases they do not—he or she can sail smoothly through the biometric borders. The 2010 killing of a senior Palestinian Hamas leader in Dubai by Israeli secret agents makes this point clear. To travel to Dubai, the agents used fake passports containing stolen identities of ordinary European and Australian citizens that had visited Israel in the past. At least one passport, issued in Germany, was confirmed to be a biometric one that had been legally obtained in 2009 by an Israeli agent using fake feeder documents (Bednarz et al. 2010).

Most important, the problem of embodied bordering goes well beyond technical concerns with national security and personal privacy, as significant as these may be. At stake here is redefining the relationships between social life, power, and space. The work of the late philosopher Michel Foucault (1977, 1978, 2007, 2008) has provided productive analytical grounding for scholarship seeking to understand the impacts that border securitization practices have on social relations (Amoore 2009; Epstein 2007; Salter 2006). Foucault's analyses of strategies of power that unearthed the connections between power, knowledge, and space remain highly relevant in the current context (Dobson and Fisher 2007). Particularly insightful are his concepts of governmentality and biopolitics that illustrate how in modern states providing security has become a form of governing populations, and how such governing is performed through the management of populations' biological characteristics, behaviors, and movements (Dillon and Lobo-Guerrero 2008; Elden 2007b).

In the twenty-first century, power is increasingly derived by securing populations. Making state borders part of everyday life as a means to securing it means acquiring power to order everyday lives. Biometrics and RFID technologies, together with the entire technological arsenal available for border enforcement, are contemporary tools used to render populations knowable by statistically classifying them along preestablished criteria, calculating their behavior in terms of risk assessment, and tracking their movements. Biometrics and RFID technologies' preoccupation with acquiring comprehensive knowledge about every mobile body that crosses state borders is a power strategy for controlling the fluid and networked territoriality of movement. Classifying bodies in terms of good versus bad mobility creates categories that are then amenable to risk contingency calculus. In this way, knowledge of the body results in power over the body. This is, at the same time, power over the most intimate and mobile of spaces.

Risk management systems such as ATS and ABC have shattered such inside/outside distinctions as citizens and noncitizens, criminals and innocents, and illegal and legal immigrants. Moreover, they combine data from government and nongovernment sources (Amoore and de Goede 2008). The goal of these technologies of power is not to differentiate between political subjects, but to get the data from the body. The identity of the body really does not matter beyond its flesh, blood, and bone existence. The body in this techno-logic of power is the kind of body as a living organism, to be kept alive to be governed, not the political body, with rights and duties, to be the subject of government (Epstein 2007).

While not being able to actually say who one really is, biometric and wireless technologies are in fact producing one's identity to say who one must be (Amoore 2006). This is essentially an imagined identity. The identity that emerges out of algorithmic calculations of personal risk profiles is not synonymous with a person's identity, which emerges over time from processes like interpersonal communication and self-reflection (van der Ploeg 1999b). This is not the identity of a person as a social being, but the identity of an object that has been rendered knowable. Instead of verifying that "you are who you say you are," the purpose changes so that "you are who we say you are." Implied here is the promise that these technologies can predict how one will behave in the future based on past patterns of behavior. The question that arises now, however, is who decides what constitutes good and bad behavior? How does one know which are good friendships to have or what is the right food to order on a plane, and which ones will increase their risk score at the border? The fact is that the data in a database can be made to tell multiple stories about a person according to what type of information the algorithmic software is programmed to look for. The algorithm defines good and bad citizens according to how it is written. As the criteria by which the algorithm works are kept secret and can change with the powers that be, the politics of biometrics become crucially important going forward (van der Ploeg 1999b). The concern is that without an understanding of what these new technologies of power can and cannot do, bordering practices may incorporate racial, class, ethnic, or gender stereotypes and prejudices that perpetuate existing inequalities.

State borders have always been "spaces of exception" with regard to the law (Salter 2004, 2006). People who have done nothing wrong automatically become suspects when they cross state borders. At the border, people find themselves in the position of perpetual suspect as they have to prove their innocence every time they cross. Today, the proof of innocence is extracted from people's bodies, which have become the new passports, IDs, and passwords. As state borders are increasingly found everywhere in everyday life, the state of permanent suspicion experienced at the border can end up becoming a generalized condition of human existence that our bodies have to clear time after time and place after place as we go about our daily routines.

6

Bridging Borders

THE CROSS-BORDER COOPERATION PARADIGM

Cross-border or transborder cooperation is a response to the limitations of state border lines in negotiating global mobilities. It consists of a series of processes and practices that seek to enhance border permeability in order to address challenges that border lines pose to surrounding areas and to the circulation of flows. Accordingly, neighboring local, regional, and national actors engage in multifaceted cooperation across borders in order to find mutually beneficial solutions to common problems that cannot be effectively addressed in a national framework. The primary goal is to transcend the barrier function of borders to allow the functional integration of neighboring borderlands. These practices first appeared in Europe in the 1960s, and by the 1990s they had become an integral part of the EU integration process. Globalization flows have engendered the emergence of such processes in other parts of the world as well, from North America and Southeast Asia to Africa and South America. Today, it is common for international treaties to include provisions for cross-border cooperation and for political leaders to express their support for these practices.

Cross-border cooperation processes taking place at the local and regional scale are inextricably linked with the broader transnational dynamics of de- and reterritorialization and de- and rebordering. To a significant extent, the success of cross-border cooperation in becoming an established governance practice during the 1990s owes much to the prevalence of the neoliberal-inspired "open borders" discourse at the time. In addition, geopolitical circumstances such as the removal of the world's main ideological "border curtains" at the end of the Cold War have also provided essential opportunity structures for the growth of cross-border cooperation (Jonsson et al. 2000; Perkmann and Sum 2002). The liberalization of border-crossing regimes through cross-border cooperation was very much in line with the spirit of these global developments.

After the attacks of September 11, 2001, security concerns have adversely affected cross-border cooperation practices, mainly in North America and at the external borders of the European Union. Stricter visa requirements along with other security-associated restrictions on mobility have proved difficult to reconcile with the logic of border bridging. The overall effect has been a decrease in the intensity of cross-border cooperation. Nonetheless, it would be incorrect to assume that border securitization is eradicating cross-border cooperation. First, the latter has always included the former. The two paradigms have never been mutually exclusive, despite their territorial logics being often contradictory. Second, the rationale behind border bridging remains intact in the twenty-first century. Third, cross-border cooperation regimes in South America, Asia, and Africa are much less affected by current border securitization practices due to their different characteristics. What has happened in the post-9/11 era is that border securitization has changed opportunity structures for cross-border cooperation. The latter is adapting by becoming a more regulated and more geographically, socially, politically, and economically selective process.

Cross-border cooperation has significantly impacted the territorial aspects of border making. It has led to the development of new territorial patterns of social interaction across borders that have opened up new spaces for the organization of social life (Popescu 2008). Put differently, cross-border cooperation is producing its own territoriality and in doing so is reterritorializing state borders. Border bridging affects interstate relations, regional identity, personal identification, cultural and social landscapes, and the political organization of space. This process raises critical questions about the nature of these cross-border spaces, their relationship with existing national and supranational spaces, and their role in reconfiguring state borders.

PUTTING SPACE BACK INTO BORDERS

Cross-border cooperation has directed considerable attention to borderlands. It is this form of border territoriality, with its sense of territorial depth and transitional character, that emerges out of cross-border cooperation practices. Bridging state borders at the subnational level implies stretching border functions across neighboring regions. This process actively incorporates borderlands into border-making strategies, thus shifting the focus from understanding the characteristics of physical border lines to understanding social interactions across the territories neighboring border lines. In this light, cross-border cooperation can be made sense of in terms of processes such as region building, regionalism, and regional governance. These are relevant to cross-border cooperation because they can take place despite the existence of borders. In this case they can lead to the emergence of cross-border regions, cross-border regionalism, cross-border institutions, and cross-border multilevel governance networks, whose aim of integrating neighboring borderlands and building cross-border communities can ultimately reterritorialize state borders (Blatter 2003; Kramsch 2001, 2003; Leresche and Saez 2002; Perkmann 1999, 2003, 2007a; Popescu 2008; Scott 1999, 2000; Sidaway 2001; Sparke 2002a).

Regions are identifiable territories of various sizes. Traditionally, regions have been taken for granted as naturally occurring territorial containers for social life. Currently, regions are seen as socially produced territories that are part of a broader network of political, economic, and cultural processes of production of space (Allen et al. 1998; MacLeod and Jones 2001; Storper 1995; Thrift 1990, 1991, 1993). Regions emerge through complex processes that combine the routine interactions of people and institutions in a territory with the influence of actors situated outside the region (Paasi 2002; Thrift 1983). They are both outcomes of and foundations for social interaction in space. Regions acquire their territorial identity through a gradual process of establishment in the public consciousness (Paasi 1996). They do not exist within neatly delineated borders; rather they are often fuzzy, overlapping, and temporal constructions.

Regionalism is a political phenomenon where local as well as nonlocal actors try to mobilize regional features for a variety of endeavors. In the Cold War era, regionalism was generally a top-down enterprise where national governments carried out various regional development policies in an attempt to improve the economic and political management of the national territory (Keating 1995, 1998). During the 1990s, when regions started to be increasingly regarded as the basis for economic, political, and social life in globalization, regionalism was reconceptualized as an emergent, bottom-up process that emerges from local actors (Keating 1995; Storper 1997). The new regionalist agenda has often been presented in terms of economic restructuring, emphasizing the significance of the so-called soft assets of a region—such as embedded social networks, local environment, regional knowledge, and cultural assets—for achieving competitive advantage in a world of flows (Painter 2002). Other aspects of the new regionalism, like the intensified competition for investments between regions as well as regional demands for political autonomy, have been generally less emphasized (Harvie 1994).

The increased importance of regions as a level of territorial organization has raised the issue of regional governance (Bukowski et al. 2003; Le Gales and Lequesne 1998). Regional governance provides a bond between territories and the institutions that organize social life, as it takes place through institutions capable of articulating regional networks of interests. These are normally multiscalar networks that can include local, national, and supranational actors and are structurally different from the hierarchical territorial-administrative structure of typical regional governments (G. Marks 1996). Thus, the common belief is that new institutions of governance are required to manage current regionalization processes (Schulz et al. 2001; Telò 2001). The capacity of these multiscalar governance institutions to successfully establish, organize, and maintain authority over territory can transform regions into meaningful political and economic actors (Le Gales 1998).

Making Cross-Border Regions

Cross-border cooperation is not a new phenomenon. The building of large cross-border infrastructure projects such as hydroelectric dams, the joint exploitation of natural resources, and the management of environmental pollution, for example, have always necessitated a degree of cross-border interaction to ease the barrier role of the border. However, this phenomenon was primarily the competence of national governments, and it is better captured by the term "intergovernmental cooperation." Much of this issue-specific cooperation has taken place through institutions such as intergovernmental commissions stuffed with national politicians or national experts and has lacked a clearly demarcated territorial framework (Blatter 2001).

Current cross-border cooperation practices depart from this model, allowing subnational authorities and civil society actors to engage in direct collaboration with their neighboring partners in what amounts to more than mere contacts across borders. This is a process of territorial integration that includes identifying cooperation priorities, defining strategies, setting agendas, and building institutions in an attempt to create a sense of cohesiveness and interdependence between divided borderlands (Scott 2000, 2002). The territorial outcomes can range from coexistent borderlands characterized by sporadic contacts across borders that barely go beyond the scope of intergovernmental cooperation to complex forms of integrated borderlands characterized by thick social interactions (Jessop 2002).

Cross-border regions are currently the most common and complex territorial frameworks for cross-border cooperation (see figure 6.1). They

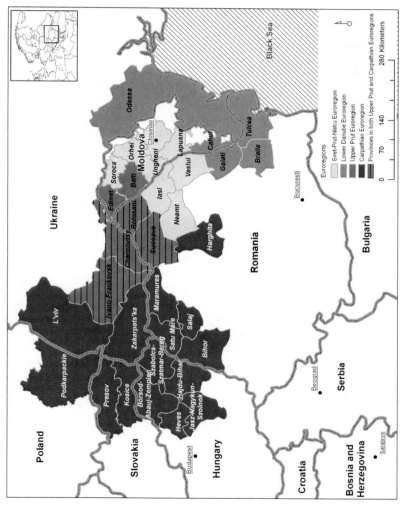

Figure 6.1 Cross-border regions in Europe. Drawn from Gabriel Popescu, "Conflicting Logics of Cross-Border Reterritorialization: Geopolitics of Euroregions in Eastern Europe," *Political Geography* 27, no. 4 (2008): 418–438, with permission from Elsevier.

are territorial units spanning two or more state borders, where social relations can be organized irrespective of state borders to the benefit of civil
society (A. Murphy 1993; Perkmann and Sum 2002). The most advanced,
typically found in Europe, can have formal governing institutions such
as councils, secretariats, and working groups as well as symbols such as
logos and flags. Their territorial shape and their borders typically emerge
from stitching together the existing national administrative subdivisions in the participating borderlands. Other, less elaborate cross-border
regions can be rather limited in scope and rely on more informal cross-
border contacts with unclear territorial shape.

Much of the enthusiasm underscoring cross-border region building
has been driven by their border-bridging potential. Economically, they
offer opportunities for enhancing the material development of borderlands by allowing economic actors to take advantage of resources situated on both sides of the border. Culturally, cross-border regions can
break down negative stereotypes that borderland inhabitants often have
about each other by promoting good neighborly relations. Politically,
they can enhance local democracy by bringing decision making closer to
the borderland inhabitants and by helping to reduce tensions between
states by keeping them engaged in constructive negotiations. Ecologi-
cally, they can provide essential frameworks for managing various environmental issues. To achieve such objectives, cross-border cooperation
in these regions faces the considerable task of developing integrative
mind-sets among a variety of local and regional actors to allow them to
identify shared interests necessary for creating common spaces of living
(van Houtum 2002).

Subnational actors are usually not subjects of international law, and
they lack the right to conclude international treaties with their counter-
parts in neighboring countries. To compensate for these disadvantages,
cross-border cooperation often involves informal or "quasi-juridical"
arrangements among the participating actors. This has often led to cross-
border cooperation being regarded as a case of "paradiplomacy" (Duchacek 1986) where local governments, and to a lesser extent private
stakeholders, develop and maintain direct cross-border contacts circumventing central governments. Nonetheless, these practices do not entirely
bypass the central governments, as they often require the involvement of
nonlocal actors. While some authors correctly stress the horizontal (i.e.,
among borderland actors) aspect of cross-border cooperation (Jonsson
et al. 2000), a more accurate understanding of this phenomenon must
take into account the vertical and interscalar aspects as well. Top-down,
bottom-up, and transversal connections coexist in these spaces. Accordingly, more elaborated cross-border cooperation schemes typically assume the form of multilevel governance networks that can involve local,

regional, and national administrations, supranational and transnational institutions, development and planning agencies, universities, private businesses, chambers of commerce, and NGOs, all interacting in a loosely coupled relationship based on coordination and negotiation rather than top-down subordination (Perkmann 1999, 2003).

In general, the formal establishment of cross-border regions includes several stages (Popescu 2011). Initially, after realizing that there are considerable mutual benefits in stimulating integration across their common borders, national governments sign bilateral or multilateral treaties where they agree to support the establishment of cross-border regions. Often these agreements also define the broad scope and the principles of cooperation, as well as the territorial makeup and the borders of cross-border regions. Supranational, transnational, and regional actors, governmental and nongovernmental alike, can be involved at this stage as well. They can provide the overarching regulatory framework, expertise, and even direct financial support, as is the case in the European Union. While this appears to be a fairly inclusive process, the decision-making power at this stage is concentrated in the hands of national leaders. This state of affairs suggests a top-down process, where national governments identify cooperation opportunities that can be taken advantage of on the other side of the border. Although this blueprint is quite common in many contexts around the world, there are also numerous situations in which local and regional actors themselves take the initiative in developing informal contacts across borders. In these cases, the intergovernmental agreements are only making official a situation that already exists on the ground.

In the second stage, the local and regional authorities normally take the front seat, defining the scope and the range of cross-border cooperation processes more specifically, writing the bylaws, identifying local projects to undertake, setting up the institutional-administrative structure of the cross-border region, and fine-tuning its territorial shape by inviting or accepting new members. This suggests a more bottom-up process at this stage, although national and supranational actors can still be included, as they hold key decision-making powers the local actors lack.

The final stage is related to management of the region. This is the stage at which most of the multilevel governance takes place, although top-down management can continue to dominate cross-border interactions in numerous situations. Multilevel governance is tedious work and involves a vast amount of coordination and negotiation among actors situated at different scales of government, in the public and private sectors, as well as across borders. For example, major cross-border cooperation projects such as the transportation infrastructure need to have on board both local and national authorities from each side of the border with competencies in the area of the project under consideration, as well as public and private actors from each side of the border with interests in the specific project. In the European Union, it may be the case that supranational actors also have to be directly involved in certain projects. At times, the logistics of cross-border cooperation in these regions can indeed overwhelm the end goals.

An important aspect that typically accompanies the establishment of cross-border regions has to do with making them visible to the public in order to gain acceptance as meaningful territories for organizing social life (Paasi 1996). For the most part, this involves place promotion strategies that assume cross-border regions are already-existing territories waiting to be discovered. To this end, stakeholders deploy identity discourses to present cross-border regions as cohesive, homogeneous spaces. Spatial symbols such as bridges, corridors, gateways, and growth triangles are used to emphasize imagined and actual commonalities existing between neighboring border regions, such as ethnic identity, economic interdependencies, and environmental concerns, in order to make cross-border regions appear as appropriate territorial frameworks for addressing these issues or for taking advantage of their potential (Perkmann and Sum 2002; Sparke 2002a).

The drawback of this approach is that it sees the emergence of cross-border regions as independent of social action, making them appear disconnected from the daily life of ordinary borderland citizens for whom these regions are often of limited practical consequence. Trying too hard to find cross-border homogeneity, even where this may not exist in reality, tends to ignore the fact that the border still exists and thus misses the chance to understand how it continues to shape social life in the borderlands. While it is true that cross-border cooperation has helped to revitalize well-established regions that have been disrupted by the imposition of state borders, it is also the case that the absence of a common identity has not prevented border regions from cooperating across borders (Leresche and Saez 2002). Anderson and O'Dowd (1999, 595) observed that in many instances "regional unity may derive from the use of the border to exploit, legally and illegally, funding opportunities or differentials in wages, prices and institutional norms on either side of the border." This view suggests that in order to bridge borders it is less important for cross-regions to be built on shared visions of common identity and functional interdependency. Rather, it is more important that they be built on shared pragmatism about borderlanders' interests (van Houtum and Strüver 2002).

Attempts to make sense of cross-border regions are grounded in two primary theoretical perspectives. The first sees the emergence of cross-border regions through the prism of capital accumulation in terms of new spaces where regional and national elites attempt to organize capitalist production under globalization (Jessop 2002; Sparke 2002a). The second sees them in terms of spaces of political action that can offer an avenue for borderland populations to emancipate themselves from the domination of central governments (Kramsch 2003; Scott 2000). Nonetheless, these two perspectives should not be understood as mutually exclusive, as most authors acknowledge that cross-border regions are shaped somewhere between the structuring effects of capitalist accumulation strategies and the agency of local and regional actors (Kramsch 2003; O'Dowd 2002a; Perkmann 2007a, 2007b; Scott 2000; Sparke 2002a, 2002b).

The cross-border literature reflects this position in several ways. Studies inspired by economics and political economy are concerned for the most part with the effects of borders on borderland economies and with understanding how economic assets in cross-border regions are incorporated into global production flows (Perkmann and Sum 2002). The goal here is to determine whether these territories can make meaningful economic actors. Scholarship influenced by political science seeks to examine the emergence of cross-border institutions and to document a certain measure of autonomy of cross-border governance networks from the state administrations. If this can be determined, it would suggest a role for cross-border regions as spaces for democratic political organization beyond the state (Kramsch 2007). Research informed by geopolitics and political geography investigates the role played by territoriality in the making of cross-border regions and seeks to understand how these territories fit in with the strategies of international power politics (Popescu 2008; Sidaway 2001). Should they prove to be more than territorial tools used by states and other actors to further their interests, this would imply a breach in the bundling of state sovereignty, territory, and borders at a cross-border level and suggest a place for cross-border regions as novel political-territorial actors in the international system. Lastly, work influenced by anthropology and sociology generally takes a cultural perspective on cross-border regions. The main thrust here is to understand the influence of state borders on group identity formation and to examine how state borders in these spaces are negotiated in daily life practices (Donnan and Wilson 1999, 2003). These insights can show whether territorial belonging in cross-border regions transcends border-based us-versus-them thinking. Common to these multi- and interdisciplinary approaches is the preoccupation with understanding the multifaceted nature of cross-border spaces and the roles they play in the territorial organization of social relations under globalization.

The experience accumulated through the functioning of cross-border regions over the last two decades makes a compelling case against simplistic understandings of border bridging as an intrinsically desirable phenomenon that reterritorializes state borders. Not all actors with a stake in state borders see potential benefits in the establishment of cross-border regions. Some see in them negative possibilities that can work against their interests. Therefore they resist them or try to keep them under control. Evidence shows that the relationship between region formation and state borders remains in a state of tension, as the latter retain considerable influence over patterns of social interaction in space. The persistence of national specificity among numerous actors involved in cross-border cooperation has generally prevented cross-border regions from reaching their full potential as meaningfully integrated spaces of living. At the core of the matter is a conflict between two territorial logics of power that has proved difficult to transcend. Cross-border regions imply territorial integration across borders. For this to happen, border bridging is essential. State borders are fundamentally disruptive here. Nation-states, on the other hand, revolve around a border containment territorial logic. For them, the importance of borders is paramount. These conflicting logics make nation-states and cross-border regions appear in competition over territory. For this reason, the degree to which nation-states tolerate cross-border territorial integration has been largely dependent on their perceptions of sovereignty loss in the borderlands. Going forward, it may take less strict emphasis on the territorial aspects of both states and cross-border regions in order to resolve the current state of tension. Nonetheless, while cross-border region making has not formally abolished any state borders so far, its overall impact has been to unsettle the long-established meaning of state borders as ultimate lines of defense and to accommodate increased connection capabilities across neighboring borderlands.

Geopolitical and Geoeconomic Cross-Border Cooperation Contexts

At a global scale, cross-border cooperation is a highly uneven process. While border-bridging schemes can be identified on virtually all continents (save Antarctica), their nature, scope, scale, and territorial frameworks present great geographical variation. To a significant extent, this variation is explained by the fact that cross-border cooperation processes are embedded into broader border regimes that provide the overarching regulatory framework for cross-border interaction (Blatter 2003). These regimes are often emerging out of regional trade blocs such as the EU, NAFTA, ASEAN, Mercosur, and others. At the same time, there is also large variation in cross-border cooperation outcomes within continents, pointing to more localized influences on border bridging. This means that the territorial outcomes of cross-border cooperation throughout the world are considerably influenced by the national and subnational political-economic institutional contexts in which they operate. To help make sense of these differences, this section sets out to offer a brief examination of several important cross-border cooperation contexts and their implications for border reterritorialization.

Europe

Europe is host to some of the oldest and most complex forms of cross-border cooperation, characterized by clearly defined territorial frameworks and formal public-sector institutions with comprehensive policies covering multiple aspects of social life. Historically, cross-border cooperation in Europe was driven primarily by political rationales and complemented by economic and cultural considerations. European integration has provided the overarching context from the beginning. In this sense, the European experience of cross-border cooperation is unique among world regions. The imagining of the European territory as a cohesive space representing more than the sum of its member states' territories has underscored the need for a regional decision-making tier to complement supranational and national institutions. In 1975, the European Union officially adopted a well-funded regional policy aimed at reducing economic disparities among various regions of Europe and allowing regional representatives to participate in European decision making to enhance grassroots democracy (Hegg and Ossenbrugge 2002; Keating 1998). Border regions have occupied a special position in the context of this policy. They have been seen as partners in the European integration process that can increase the cohesiveness of the EU territory by overcoming the divisive role of state borders through cross-border integration.

The specific reasons behind European cross-border cooperation vary with time. The first steps took place in the 1950s and were part of Franco-German reconciliation efforts involving informal cross-border contacts between local authorities (Anderson and Bort 2001; O'Dowd and Wilson 1996). Subsequently, an early area of cross-border cooperation seeking to address issues of uneven economic development took shape along the western borders of Germany, involving the Netherlands, Belgium, France, and Switzerland. In the 1980s, cross-border cooperation acquired a new sense of purpose in preparation for the creation of the Single Market, which required a common European space for the free movement of goods, people, capital, and ideas. This culminated with the abolition of border controls in much of the European Union after the implementation of the Schengen Agreement in 1997. These developments ushered in a period of denationalization of borders that shifted the emphasis on their functions as gateways and resources to symbolize the capacity of connecting people and forging common identities across state borders (O'Dowd 2002b).

During the 1990s, cross-border cooperation became one of the most dynamic areas of EU regional policy (Christiansen and Jorgenson 2000). By the late 1990s, there was not a single border in the European Union that was not covered by some type of cross-border cooperation scheme. In this context, cross-border regions, commonly known in Europe as Euroregions or "Euregios," emerged as the most common form of institutionalized cross-border cooperation. Kepka and Murphy (2002) have argued that Euroregions have come to describe any substate cooperation framework that has a cross-border character irrespective of its organizational structure. The first Euroregions appeared in the late 1950s in the Dutch-German borderlands and were primarily the outcome of bottom-up social action aimed at addressing issues of marginalization generated by nation-state borders. However, their number increased greatly after 1990, reaching over one hundred. In 2004, they accounted for almost 50 percent of EU territory and comprised about 10 percent of its population (Ferrera 2004).

For the last two decades, various EU institutions have been actively involved in promoting and supporting the establishment of Euroregions as part of a broader strategy of functional territorial integration. To this end, the European Union set up several cross-border cooperation funding programs, among which INTERREG has been by far the most influential. Since its initiation in 1990, the INTERREG budget has totaled over fifteen billion euros. These EU funds have had a profound structuring effect on the development of Euroregions, shaping their cooperation priorities to a significant degree. Funding has been predominantly oriented toward projects of economic development such as transportation and communication infrastructure. Other important spheres have included environmental protection, cultural exchanges, health care, education, and tourism (Jonsson et al. 2000). However, significant aspects of daily life in border regions, such as labor, leisure, social programs, and others, have ranked low on the list of funding priorities.

Cross-border cooperation after 1990 has also played a significant role in the EU enlargement strategy of integrating East European applicant countries. The EU policy makers came to see the Euroregions as a territorial framework where East Europeans would prepare for EU membership by practicing multilevel governance, by learning to address border-related issues cooperatively, and by working to reduce cross-border economic asymmetries (Scott 2000; Yoder 2003). In this way, the EU "space" of cross-border cooperation was extended to Eastern Europe before any of the countries in the region gained EU membership.

It is difficult to determine a typical model of a Euroregion as there is wide variation in their shape, nature, and functioning. However, there are some common features. Many Euroregions are organized among cross-border municipalities or regions, their size ranges from fifty to one hundred kilometers in width, they are inhabited by a few million people, and they have a well-defined organizational structure (Perkmann 2003). They often share cultural characteristics and ethnic populations that constitute minorities in one state or another. Some Euroregions have achieved notable results with regard to border bridging. One example is the Maas-Rhine Euroregion that straddles Belgium, Germany, and the Netherlands. It has a population of 3.6 million inhabitants who share the Dutch, Flemish, Walloon, and German languages and cultures. The Euroregion has its own governing body with authority over financial matters, and a Euroregional Council with consultative functions that serves as a parliament. Its members meet twice a year and belong to political parties and nongovernmental associations like labor unions, chambers of commerce, and universities (Kramsch 2001). Other Euroregions have achieved less remarkable results, functioning mainly as tools for the national governments and local authorities to tap EU funds.

Currently, the European Union operates with two sets of border regimes that have far-reaching consequences for the reterritorialization of borders on the continent. While inside the European Union state borders have been bridged in the sense that they are not physical obstacles to movement any longer, the EU's external borders have become major barriers, particularly with regard to the movement of people. Cultural and economic factors have gained renewed importance in defining who belongs and who does not belong in Europe, who are Europe's Others. Countries situated east and south of the external borders have been depicted in European geopolitical discourse as outsiders with little to no foreseeable chance of EU membership. Subsequent border-making practices such as increased border policing and the hardening of the visa regime appear to confirm this stance. Specifically, restrictive EU visa policies have created apprehension among EU neighbors that "paper curtains" are being erected between them and the European Union (Apap and Tchorbadjiyska 2004).

External EU borderlands have emerged as sites where perceived security threats to stability in the EU space, such as immigration, organized crime, drugs, and human trafficking, can be contained and addressed (Anderson and Bort 2001; van Houtum 2002). EU policy makers attempt to walk a tightrope between including their neighbors as embodied in their discourse on cross-border cooperation, and excluding them as embodied in their discourse on securitizing their outer borders. In 2003, the European Union launched the European Neighborhood Policy (ENP), which aimed to create a framework for comprehensive partnership between the European Union and its East and South European neighbors. Cross-border cooperation, backed by funds of over one billion euros, constitutes a major strategy of the ENP (Batt 2003). Euroregions are once again playing an important role in supporting cross-border cooperation along the external borders of the European Union. They serve as territorial interfaces between EU and non-EU space. While formally the European Union stops at its external borders, informally the Euroregions' territory is tantamount to a territorial overlapping between EU and non-EU space. These Euroregions are expected to achieve the same goals as those existing inside EU space, yet under the contradictory circumstances of offsetting issues emerging from increasing the barrier function of the external EU borders. Cross-border cooperation along the European Union's external borders is less concerned with integrating daily life across borderlands and more focused on addressing EU interests in these borderlands. In many ways, the interpersonal relations in the Romanian-Ukrainian Euroregions, for example, were more vigorous before Romania became an EU member than after. It is difficult to do meaningful border bridging when borderland inhabitants are denied steady and spontaneous movement across the border. Borderland inhabitants have responded to these new border realities in ways that attempt to amend them to better suit their interests. These have included immigrating illegally to the European Union in larger numbers than before, seeking legal residence in the European Union for extended periods of time, and applying for citizenship in neighboring EU countries (Berg and Ehin 2006; Popescu 2008).

North America

North American cross-border cooperation is characterized by loosely defined territorial frameworks and less formal institutional arrangements with limited policy goals (Blatter 2001; Scott 2002). There is no supranational or national policy framework for borderland integration and no systematic coordination between central governments and borderland authorities regarding cross-border cooperation objectives. Cross-border cooperation tends to focus on specific issues rather than forming a comprehensive strategy for the management of social life in the borderlands. At the same time, cross-border cooperation practices have been generally open to the participation of private actors and to the establishment of public-private partnerships as a way to compensate for the reduced level of support local authorities receive from the central governments (Norman and Bakker 2009; Scott 1999).

Cross-border cooperation in North America has been historically driven by economic rationales, followed at a distance by environmental and cultural considerations. In the north, the fact that 90 percent of Canada's population lives within 150 miles of the 5,525-mile (8,891 km) U.S.-Canada border constitutes a major incentive for cross-border cooperation.

In the south, across the 1,969-mile (3,169 km) U.S.-Mexico border, cooperation incentives come from the unequal levels of development between
the two countries. North American borderlands also share strong cultural
ties. The southern U.S. borderland was part of Mexico prior to 1848 and
today is inhabited by a significant number of people of Hispanic/Latino
heritage. The U.S.-Canada borderlands share, for the most part, the Anglo
cultural affinity as both countries were part of the British Empire. These
circumstances help explain why, despite the weakness of formal integration projects in the borderlands, cross-border interaction at the level of
civil society has been particularly strong across both the U.S.-Canada and
the U.S.-Mexico borders. Each year several hundred million people cross
these two borders for work, education, tourism, family visits, and shop-
ping, spending billions of dollars in the borderlands and beyond (Payan
and Vasquez 2007; Ramos 2007). We need to add here the equally strong
illegal cross-border interactions that can range from drug and arms trafficking to people smuggling.

Generally, North American borderlands have been seen by the central
governments and by numerous entrepreneurs as territories that can be
used to improve the global competitiveness of North American businesses
in a "free trade" context. There are several cross-border regions where
cooperation concentrates. We mention here only a few, such as Cascadia
(centered on Seattle and Vancouver) and Detroit–Windsor, across the U.S.-
Canada border, and San Diego–Tijuana, Arizona–Sonora, and El Paso–Ciu-
dad Juarez, across the U.S.-Mexico border (Alper 1996; Konrad and Nicol
2008; Wong-Gonzales 2004). While cooperation in these regions involves a
range of issues, from the environment to education, in many respects the
economic integration of these borderlands can be considered the most successful aspect of border bridging on the continent. This process gathered
momentum after the 1960s, when numerous U.S. manufacturing firms
moved their assembly facilities (maquiladoras) south of the border to take
advantage of the cheap labor in the Mexican borderlands. At the same time,
the U.S. automotive industry established intrafirm supply chains for auto
parts in the Canadian borderlands. Much of this cross-border production
operated in a just-in-time production environment, which demanded that
waiting time at the border be reduced to a minimum.

The signing of NAFTA in 1993 boosted the existing economic cooperation in the borderlands and significantly expanded cross-border trade to
include services, agricultural products, and other sectors. However, this
expansion should not be understood as a border-bridging success in creating common spaces of living. Despite being crossed by huge volumes of
traffic, state borders continue to divide borderland societies. Borderland
inhabitants have been unequally affected by the benefits of economic integration, and the economic achievements have not been replicated in other

spheres of social life. Moreover, a significant proportion of the wealth created by this economic integration leaves the borderlands to benefit other
locations in the interior.

Other key issues that have long framed formal cross-border cooperation in North America are immigration and the drug trade. The U.S.-Mex-
ico borderlands in particular have experienced a border regime of gradual
strengthening after World War I (save for economic matters) as part of
the U.S. government's strategy for coping with these issues (Andreas
2000; Nevins 2002). During the last one hundred years, the U.S.-Mexico
border has transitioned from un-demarked and unguarded to one of the
most fenced and policed borders in the world. Yet illegal immigration and
drug trafficking have increased unabated during this time. In stark contrast, the U.S.-Canada border came to be seen as "the longest undefended
border in the world," reflecting the popular perception of a "friction-free"
U.S.-Canada intergovernmental relationship. After the 2000s, however,
the peaceful perception of this lightly policed border has changed to one
of potential security risk for the United States.

The attacks of September 11, 2001, radically transformed the cross-
border cooperation context in North America, mostly by limiting its scope
and changing its priorities (Payan and Vasquez 2007). While overall trade
levels between the United States, Canada, and Mexico have continued
to grow since 2001, the same thing cannot be said of the overall border-
bridging process. After 2001, security concerns trumped all integration
arguments. The U.S. government has applied a one-size-fits-all border
security policy that has ignored the diversity of North American local
border contexts and increased the militarization of U.S. borders. These
developments undermined many of the integration efforts under way at
the local level, reduced the decision-making power of local authorities
in matters of cross-border cooperation, and left borderland communities without meaningful avenues for regular input into border policies
with direct impact on their livelihoods. For example, a highly evocative
incident took place in 2007 at the U.S.-Canada border when a Canadian
fire truck honoring a decades-old cross-border agreement rushed to assist
with a fire in the neighboring U.S. border village of Rouses Point, New
York (Meserve and Ahlers 2007). The Canadian fire truck was delayed at
the U.S. border checkpoint because the new security procedures required
that the border guards verify the immigration status of the Canadian
firefighters.

The main challenge for the U.S. government is to find the right balance
between "free trade" across its borders and its perceived security needs
(Brunet-Jailly 2007). During the last decade, the United States launched a
series of security-related initiatives such as "Smart Borders," the "North
American Security Perimeter," and the "Security and Prosperity Part-

nership," whose overall aim is to integrate North American security in order to achieve selective permeability for U.S. borders (Ramos 2007). To date, this strategy seems to have achieved a measure of success with regard to the fluidization of large-scale trade flows, but it has been mostly detrimental to local border-bridging processes. The latest of these initiatives, implemented in 2009 and dubbed the Western Hemisphere Travel Initiative (WHTI), is emblematic of the impacts that border securitization has on North American cross-border cooperation. The WHTI ended an era of passport-free travel to Canada, Mexico, and the Caribbean for U.S. citizens as well as passport-free entry into the U.S. for Canadian citizens. Currently, U.S. citizens need to possess a passport when traveling anywhere outside U.S. borders.

Southeast Asia

In Southeast Asia, cross-border cooperation achieved considerable popularity in the early 1990s. Numerous national governments promoted the building of cross-border regions under the generic name of "growth triangles" as a strategy for promoting economic development based on a glocal logic that requires the creation of regional competitiveness within a global context (Sparke et al. 2004; Sum 2002). As a consequence, many growth triangles can be seen in terms of cross-border export-processing zones that are closely linked to the broader East Asian export-oriented development strategy and are essentially driven by economic rationales.

Cross-border cooperation in these areas includes both public and private networks of actors, as well as public-private partnerships. However, cross-border interactions have minimal formal institutionalization and are largely dominated by state actors with minor involvement from local authorities (Grundy-Warr 2002). Cross-border integration at the subnational level has not been on the official agenda, as growth triangles are generally set up to benefit the national interests of each constitutive part. By far the best known example of a cross-border region in Southeast Asia is the Indonesia-Malaysia-Singapore Growth Triangle. This has been established mainly as a means to expanding the hinterland of the city-state of Singapore. Malaysian and Indonesian leaders have sought to benefit from investment spillovers from the much wealthier Singaporean economy (Sparke et al. 2004). Other examples of cross-border regions include the Greater Mekong Subregion, between Vietnam, Cambodia, Laos, and Thailand, as well as the "northern triangle" between Malaysia, Thailand, and Indonesia. In addition to these formal projects, many informal cross-border regions are not subsumed by any formal "growth triangle" initiative.

South America

During the last two decades, supranational integration projects such as Mercosur and the Andean Community have provided the backdrop for very dynamic cross-border interactions in South America. However, to date the direct impact of these trade blocs on subnational cross-border cooperation has been rather limited, as they remain intergovernmental organizations with relatively weak institutions (Dupeyron 2009). Supranational integration has indeed opened up national borders to interregional and global trade, but has benefited to a lesser extent cross-border integration at the level of civil society (Amilhat-Szary 2003; Hevilla and Zusman 2009).

Throughout South America, there are numerous local cross-border initiatives, projects, and organizations that include both private and public actors (Machado et al. 2009). Economic goals predominate, but environmental and education-related rationales may also be present. Generally the implementation of cross-border cooperation schemes is largely dependent on state actors and on interstate relations. There are many borderlands with active informal cooperation or with a weak degree of institutionalized cooperation. More formal cross-border regions can be found in the borderlands of Brazil, Paraguay, and Argentina surrounding Iguaçu Falls, as well as in the borderlands between Chile, Peru, and Bolivia, centered on the cities of Arica, Chile, and Tacna, Peru.

Recent developments in supranational integration like the establishment of the Union of South American Nations (UNASUR) in 2008, which includes twelve South American countries, appear to present additional opportunities for deepening cross-border cooperation. One particularly important outcome of the UNASUR establishment has been the decision to eliminate the use of passports by the nationals of South American countries for traveling between those countries. This decision comes very close to achieving the free movement of people across the continent. Today it is possible for a citizen of one South American country to travel with a national ID card from one tip of the continent to another, from Caracas, Venezuela, to Ushuaia, Argentina. To put this achievement into perspective, suffice it to mention that it comes at a time when the United States has just introduced passport-based border crossing with its neighbors, and the European Union has tightened its visa policies for the citizens of its neighboring countries.

Africa

Cross-border cooperation in Africa is framed to a considerable extent by the postcolonization context in which formal state borders have less impact than ethnicity and religion on the perpetuation of group identity. Informal interactions across rarely enforced African state borders have been a fact of life for a long time. Starting in the 1990s, there have been attempts to institutionalize some of these informal areas of cooperation. These attempts have been rooted in neoliberal practices that have sought to pool local resources across borders in order to favorably position certain African regions vis-à-vis global investment flows (Soderbaum and Taylor 2008). Top-down cooperation initiatives predominate, with public policies creating favorable conditions for private and foreign investments.

A major issue in the development of cross-border regions in Africa is that the continent's postcolonial states are generally too weak to formalize cross-border interactions to a significant degree. Thus numerous formal cooperation initiatives are taken over by state elites that use them to extract benefits, which are then distributed to a network of political clients that help maintain these elites in power (Soderbaum and Taylor 2008). In these circumstances, cross-border cooperation at the level of civil society continues to remain highly informal. Among the more active cross-border regions are the Maputo Development Corridor that links Johannesburg, South Africa, with the port of Maputo, Mozambique; the Zambia-Malawi-Mozambique Growth Triangle; and the tourism-driven Victoria Falls region between Zambia and Zimbabwe.

The Middle East

In the Middle East, the authoritarian nature of many regimes that favor political centralization, together with the regional consequences of the ongoing Israeli-Palestinian conflict, has left little room for the intergovernmental trust building necessary for allowing local authorities the decision-making autonomy to engage in cross-border cooperation. Official discourses in this region continue to stress the defense functions of borders despite the potential benefits cross-border cooperation could bring to the lives of borderland inhabitants.

To date, there are no formal cross-border regions in the Middle East. Nonetheless, there are several border segments where active informal cross-border cooperation takes place, such as between Turkey and Syria (Rabo 2006). Another example is the cooperation between the Red Sea coastal cities of Eilat, Israel, and Aqaba, Jordan. In this case, the existence of meaningful cooperative actions on environmental issues between local authorities is rarely publicized due to concerns that they would trigger severe adverse reactions from people who see this cooperation through the larger lens of the Arab-Israeli conflict (Arieli 2010).

EUROREGIONS AND THE DIMENSIONS
OF BORDER RETERRITORIALIZATION

Owing to its position as the most dynamic contemporary cross-border cooperation context, Europe offers unique insights into the possibilities and the limitations of border-bridging processes with regard to the future of interstate borders and the territorial reorganization of social relations. Euroregions are a prism through which to examine these relationships.

It is difficult to interpret with precision the influence that cross-border cooperation in Euroregions has on border reterritorialization, as the relationship between these two phenomena is not straightforward. Rather, it is influenced by the expectations that various stakeholders have of cross-border cooperation as well as by their understanding of what the role of borders should be and the meaning they attach to them. Many observers are skeptical of the Euroregions' achievements, pointing to the fact that after twenty years most of them fall short of their goal of integrating borderlands. To be sure, Euroregions have not captured people's imagination in the same way nation-states did, nor have they succeeded in becoming twenty-first-century global economic hubs (Sparke 2002a). However, caution has to be used when interpreting the failure to meet expectations as evidence of a lack of border bridging. The specific interests of the actors involved in cross-border cooperation produced a crowded agenda for Euroregions that was often contradictory. Under these circumstances, we can speak of a "burden of expectations" bestowed on Euroregions that has made their goals unrealistic (Kramsch and Hooper 2004). They were expected, among other things, to help reduce political tensions among states, to become economic engines, to foster common identity, and to manage environmental pollution. All of these rather lofty goals have come before the more modest and immediate ones related to daily life in the borderlands. Commenting on these challenges, Clement and colleagues (1999, 275) note that "Not only must border regions do everything every other region must do in terms of increasing competitiveness, but they must do so *in collaboration with* the region(s) on the other side, which is likely to be economically and politically organized very differently."

The following sections offer an interpretation of border bridging in Euroregions. Several dimensions of border change emerge from an examination of the last two decades of European cross-border cooperation, allowing for a grounded assessment of the cross-border cooperation paradigm at the beginning of the twenty-first century.

The Legal Dimension

The creation of Euroregions across the borders of European states raised legal challenges from the start. There was simply no room either in national or in international law to allow for the establishment of any sort of formal cross-border territorial entities. National laws ended at the borders of states, and international laws regulated mainly interstate relations. There was no legal basis for cross-border agreements between subnational authorities from neighboring states. Subnational authorities were traditionally banned from engaging in international law that was reserved only for the national authorities. In these conditions, the legal framework required for making cross-border spaces had to be created from scratch.

Initially, Euroregions were established on the basis of informal agreements that relied mostly on the goodwill of those involved in their functioning, or in some cases on private law arrangements. The typical form of Euroregion establishment was the "twin association," where municipalities or regional authorities formed an association on each side of the border in concordance with their own national legal system, and later, in a subsequent step, they joined each other on the basis of a cross-border agreement to establish a Euroregion (Perkmann 2003). Given their quasi-formal legal status, for many Euroregions it was difficult to even have a common bank account. Finances had to be managed from separate accounts on each side of the border. For cross-border cooperation to develop, a more reliable legal framework was needed, ideally anchored in the public law domain. As Euroregions often straddle two or more systems of national law, the challenge was to create a legal status that would be valid on all sides of a border (Baker 1996). However, a uniform cross-border legal status had the potential to put into question the legal notion of border-defined state national sovereignty.

The first major steps toward the creation of a public law–based legal framework for the functioning of Euroregions were spearheaded by the Council of Europe, which subscribed to a legal understanding of Euroregions as formal political-administrative entities (Perkmann 2003). In 1980, these efforts resulted in the passing of the European Outline Convention on Transfrontier Cooperation between Territorial Communities and Authorities, better known as the Madrid Convention. On this occasion, a series of documents were adopted that provided a legal basis for cross-border cooperation among subnational authorities in areas such as regional development, environmental protection, building of infrastructure, and disaster assistance. The main aim of the Madrid Convention was to allow local authorities engaged in cross-border cooperation the same opportunities that they would have within a nation-state. An additional protocol to the Madrid Convention came into force in 1995, explicitly granting local and regional authorities the right to conclude public law cross-border cooperation agreements with the caveat that these agreements not contravene the national laws of the states involved. However, most signatory states entered a provision to the effect that specific schemes of cross-border cooperation had to be within the terms of bilateral treaties with neighboring countries (Anderson and Bort 2001). This meant that national laws continued to dictate the terms of cross-border agreements. Notwithstanding this fact, the significance of the Madrid Convention resides in the fact that it offered a legal point of reference, a precedent that opened up the European legal system to subnational cross-border actors.

By the early 1990s, several European states signed a series of bilateral and multilateral cross-border treaties, such as the Benelux Cross-Border Convention in 1989, the German-Dutch cross-border treaty in 1991, and the Karlsruhe Agreement in 1996 between Switzerland, France, Germany, and Luxembourg (Kramsch 2002a). Various Euroregions in places such as the Rhine Valley took advantage of these newly created opportunities and became public law organizations. It could be argued that they carry out some prerogatives previously reserved for sovereign states, although the decisions taken by such transnational bodies are binding only on the public authorities within the participating cross-border areas and not on the civil subjects living there (Perkmann 2003). The latter continue to remain in the exclusive realm of national law.

The emergence of a cross-border legal framework in Europe, although weak and incomplete, had significant implications for border bridging. On the one hand, the extent to which state sovereignty is threatened at the border by the implications of the legal status of Euroregions is arguable, as national laws set the parameters of cross-border agreements. On the other hand, the very existence of these cross-border territories constitutes a legal challenge for state sovereignty. They have opened up innovative ways of conceiving of juridical affairs positioned beyond the reach of the traditional legal system, at the fringes of national and international law. Anderson and Bort (2001) noticed that the constitution and legislation of many European states had to be modified to allow subnational authorities to enter treaty-like agreements with partners in other countries. They interpret this as a signal that a certain transfer of sovereignty rights at the cross-border level has already taken place in Europe.

Recent developments have taken this issue even further. In 2006, the European Commission has taken the legal initiative and has adopted a new cross-border cooperation instrument known as the European Grouping of Territorial Cooperation (EGTC). Effectively, the EGTC seeks to transcend the lack of coherence in legal matters bedeviling cross-border cooperation by grounding cross-border cooperation agreements in EU law. The EGTC allows stakeholders situated at various levels of government and in civil society to enter cross-border agreements with legally binding decisions and enables cross-border institutions to have their own budget, hire their own staff, and own property. These are all remarkable legal developments. At the same time, it must be noted that the EGTC is not tailored specifically to cross-border cooperation in the borderlands, as was the case with the Madrid Convention and its protocol. It covers any form of cooperation across borders, including inter- and transregional, as well as interstate. It has been developed with the logic of functional integration between EU places in mind, and it is of little use for cross-border cooperation at the external borders of the European Union. In other words, the EGTC is a flexible legal tool catered primarily toward assisting the larger objective of EU territorial cohesion. This may well be a broader and more radical path to border bridging inside the European Union, but it remains to be seen to what degree this process resonates with matters of practical concern in the daily life of the borderlands. So far, local authorities in Euroregions have not rushed to adopt the EGTC.

The Territorial Dimension

Establishing Euroregions involves territorial delineation across state borders. In this process, new types of territories are created—cross-border territories—that question the theoretical foundations of the existing order based on absolute territorial sovereignty inside state borders. Euroregions are territories situated outside this logic. They overlap the margins of sovereign territories, bringing them together in one single territory. Their functioning requires an effort of political-territorial imagination on the part of national, supranational, and local actors. They have to find ways to uncouple territoriality and political organization in order to defuse the subversive potential of Euroregions with regard to a state's borders and its territorial integrity.

Euroregions are supposed to acquire a certain degree of territorial-administrative autonomy vis-à-vis central governments in order to function as spaces of bottom-up governance. Central governments have to relinquish to local authorities some of their exclusive control over the governance of these territories. Here is where tensions between states and Euroregions emerge. Owing to frequent territorial changes that characterize the formation of European states, the degree of borderland assimilation into state territory varies greatly. Borderlands are often inhabited by minorities whose national allegiance has a long history of being distrusted by their central governments. In addition, Euroregions can sometimes bypass central governments and deal directly with supranational institutions in

Brussels regarding issues that central governments are unable or unwilling to negotiate. As a result, central governments have typically been very sensitive to border regions, showing guarded enthusiasm toward the establishment of formal cross-border territories with integrated governance institutions that they cannot fully control. The main concern has been that Euroregions could be used to modify state borders by detaching territories from one state and attaching them to another (Delli Zotti 1996).

At the same time, central governments normally understand the benefits Euroregions can bring to their borderlands. However, they face a complex dilemma as they have to weigh these benefits against the broader interests of the state. In this light, central governments cannot allow borderlands to pursue territorial integration strategies that are perceived to undermine state interests, even if these strategies may serve better the interests of borderland citizens. This is why central governments often attempt to undermine Euroregions even as they promote them. In situations where state and borderland interests coincide, central governments have been actively engaged in supporting border-bridging practices. Where these interests do not align well, central governments have been apprehensive of cross-border integration and have attempted to control Euroregions. The point is that central governments have been less interested in Euroregions becoming integrated territories for social life and more interested in using them as territorial frameworks for addressing domestic and intergovernmental issues. The establishment of Euroregions resembled more a national strategy for political and economic development than a grassroots demand for overcoming constrictive state borders in order to create novel spaces of living capable of better fulfilling the aspirations of borderland citizens. This geostrategic understanding of the role of Euroregions has often limited local input in the creation of Euroregions and has restricted the border-bridging effect of cross-border cooperation practices (Popescu 2008).

The European Union's outlook on Euroregions has been less ambiguous. Its territorial agenda of European integration has fit much better with cross-border integration imperatives. It was largely due to the existence of the European Union as a supranational structure that member states were able to build the high levels of mutual trust required for establishing Euroregions across their borders. However, after the reinforcement of its external borders during the 2000s, the European Union's territorial interests conflict with those of the Euroregions to such an extent that the European Union has become one of the major disruptive forces that cross-border integration along the external borders has to overcome.

The presence of Euroregions across the borders of states has important implications for the role these borders play in the territorial organization of Europe. Euroregions do not challenge state borders directly in the sense that they erase them or render them irrelevant for social interaction. There is significant consensus that Euroregions are not unified territories outside the state and EU hegemony, as their degree of political-territorial organization remains weak (Perkmann 2007b; Sparke 2002a). They do not necessarily signal the territorial fragmentation of state sovereignty, as in many cases they have emerged out of state actions to implement policies across borders (Jessop 2002). However, Euroregions do challenge state borders in the sense that they alter their functions and their territoriality. They are at odds with an understanding of state borders in terms of ultimate lines of territorial control over which states have exclusive power. The very building of territorial units across state borders signals the emergence of a process of border reterritorialization. When central governments agree to put together parts of the national territory to form a cross-border territory, they implicitly endorse a new, separate territory that is beyond the exclusive sovereign reach of any single central government. Also, when national and local administrations or nongovernmental actors participate in the institutionalization of Euroregions, the new institutions exercise authority and power, as tenuous as that might be, beyond state borders. In essence, the territory of Euroregions represents more than the sum of the state territories that compose it, and cross-border institutions are more than the sum of the national administrations forming them.

These qualities reveal that Euroregions have been shaped to a large extent by territorial considerations. They have been imagined as new territories that offer opportunities to overcome the shortcomings of the existing ones such as the states. In this, they have retained the territoriality principle as a mode of organizing social relations instead of overcoming it. Their clear territorial shape, bureaucratic institutional structure, and wide-ranging integration goals make them resemble state territorial organization, only on a smaller scale. While this characteristic has assured Euroregions a certain degree of functional stability, it has also made some stakeholders wary. An alternative path to border bridging would be to envision the territoriality of cross-border cooperation practices in terms of sets of spatial relations that emerge from the routine activities of social actors. This would have the advantage of being more sensitive to local contexts while downplaying tensions with the national state.

The Economic Dimension

One of the strongest rationales in support of Euroregions has been argued on economic grounds. There is a broad convergence of interests on the part of the cross-border cooperation stakeholders to promote economic development in the borderlands, considering their history of marginalization at the fringes of national economic systems. The need for economically integrated borderlands is genuine, and the benefits they can offer to civil society are tangible. Not surprisingly, cross-border economic integration has generated the most consensus among stakeholders. It is paradoxical, then, that this dimension is one of the areas where the least progress has been made during the last two decades.

The economic argument for the establishment of Euroregions is based mainly on a functional logic that sees state borders as obstacles that increase the costs of economic exchanges and preclude taking advantage of the complementary assets existing in neighboring borderlands (Keating 1998; Perkmann and Sum 2002). The core assumption is that the removal of barriers to economic exchanges turns borderlands' peripheral status into an advantage by making them attractive for a range of economic activities that can generate economic development. Consequently, Euroregions have been expected to become new territories where capitalist accumulation strategies can be organized to the benefit of all stakeholders (Jessop 2002).

In line with this vision, there have been several EU achievements that constitute notable opportunity structures for cross-border economic integration. These include the implementation of the Single Market which created a unified European economic space; the adoption of the Schengen Treaty which assured the free circulation of persons, capital, and goods; and the introduction of financial programs such as the INTERREG which provided direct financing for cross-border cooperation schemes. What the European Union and member states have been less willing to do is enact specific economic regulations for border regions. Tax free areas, free ports, and special economic zones are rare in the EU borderlands. At the same time, when it comes to local cross-border interactions, the lack of exceptions in economic matters misses a chance to stimulate borderland economic actors and works to keep key decision-making powers concentrated at the national and supranational levels. As a result, the opportunity structures for cross-border integration in the European Union have not proven sufficient to overcome the inertia of national economic systems of which the borderlands are a part (van der Velde and van Houtum 2004). There may be "free trade" in the European Union, but economics is much more than "free trade." Member states continue to have different economic policies and regulations that local cross-border exchanges have to negotiate daily. In this light, when considering Euroregions' economic achievements, it is important to keep in mind that they do not have the power to raise taxes or to make independent economic policies.

Generally, Euroregions have had some success in involving the public sector in cross-border economic activities such as infrastructure projects. Numerous borderlands have benefited from increased flows of investment from the EU and central governments. However, there has been limited success in generating cross-border private business networks. In many instances, smuggling and small-scale cross-border traffic remain the most integrated forms of economic exchange. The domination of cross-border cooperation structures by formal administrative institutions appears to have deterred public-private partnerships as well as large-scale private-sector participation in Euroregions (Scott 2000).

The economic argument for Euroregions has overlooked the fact that neighboring border regions that share similar economic structures do not necessarily have to cooperate once the barrier effect of the borders is removed (Keating 1998). They may choose to compete with each other if they can further their economic interests elsewhere. In places considered to be cross-border integration success stories, such as the Swiss-German-French "Regio TriRhena," the Swiss-French "Regio Genevensis," or the more recent Danish-Swedish Oresund Euroregion, development was less dependent on EU financing programs and more on local contexts such as growth pressures from the urban hinterlands of Geneva, Basel, Copenhagen, and Malmo (Sohn et al. 2009). Cross-border cooperation did not create these situations; rather it stimulated their development.

In the end, the weaker-than-expected economic performance of Euroregions may point out that other forces, outside the realm of economics, are working to undermine the emergence of economically integrated borderlands in Europe (Kramsch 2003). Cross-border economic exchanges do not follow neatly rational cost-cutting models. More contentious cultural and political factors, for example, also play a role in shaping the economic fortunes of Euroregions.

The Cultural Dimension

Cultural issues concerning Euroregions revolve around the notion of identity. Historically, states strove to create a nationally centered group identity, with their borders signifying the territorial limits of this identity. State borders functioned as markers and makers of a national identity that was understood in mutually exclusive terms. National identity left no room for shared or multiple identities. Accordingly, the inhabitants of European borderlands often had to bear intense nationalization pressures to conform to these norms. From these processes, the borders of Europe emerged as sites of intense cultural symbolism.

Euroregions straddle these culturally dysfunctional territories. They have been expected to create shared identities that can bridge the former markers of difference. The belief is that cooperation at the local scale across state borders can help develop a densely knit web of social interactions that will lead to the crystallization of cross-border identities (Perkmann and Sum 2002; Scott 2000). Moreover, in instances where self-conscious ethnic minorities inhabit the borderlands, the hope is that the establishment of Euroregions will quickly lead to the resurgence of historical territorial identities. The problem with these assumptions is that the shared identities the Euroregions are expected to foster have been perceived by some powerful stakeholders as inevitably rivaling national identities.

Bottom-up minority pressures for increased cultural autonomy, together with top-down, supranational discourses and cultural policies in support of building a European identity, did create an environment favorable to increased cultural interactions across state borders. In several places where populations with common ethnocultural backgrounds inhabit neighboring borderlands, cross-border identities seem to have materialized. In most cases, however, there is little evidence that cross-border identities have emerged (Paasi and Prokkola 2008; Strüver 2003). While direct social interaction has proven to be an effective way to confront the stereotypes people have about each other, it is also true that sometimes meeting the "Other" can simply reinforce these stereotypes (Newman 2006a). This indicates that it is too much to expect for the removal of physical barriers to social interaction to lead by itself to a common identity. The experience of Euroregions shows that borders persist in people's minds for a long time after their physical disappearance. The removal of mental borders is proving to be more difficult than anticipated, as national belonging often manifests itself in indifference vis-à-vis neighboring borderlands and low cross-border mobility among borderland inhabitants (van der Velde and van Houtum 2004). State borders remain the most important markers of identity in most Euroregions, and they are markers of difference as far as cross-border integration is concerned. Euroregion symbols, such as their names, maps, and flags, as well as their histories and aspirations reflected in the discourses of local leaders, evoke modest shared feelings when compared with well-established national symbols. The outcome is often that each borderland keeps reproducing its own national stereotypes instead of creating a common identity (Fall 2005; Strüver 2003).

Another factor that has stifled the emergence of shared identity has to do with the top-down geographical imagination of many Euroregions, which tends to lump together territories that have little in common with the cultural characteristics of borderlands. A more appropriate context for cultural integration in Euroregions can emerge by taking into consideration predominantly grassroots geographical imaginations. As the local is the closest scale at which people experience borders both in their discursive and physical forms, a grassroots-anchored pattern of cross-border interaction could create a solid base for reterritorialized identities in Euroregions.

Nonetheless, exclusive focus on the emergence of shared identities can obscure the cultural border-bridging progress that is already taking place in Euroregions. Borderland inhabitants are generally well aware of their shared interests. In many instances, cultural activities have dominated formal cross-border interactions. It has been easier to organize folk festivals than it has been to build road bridges across borders. The significance of the cultural dimension of cross-border cooperation resides not in erasing cultural differences but in helping to deal with them pragmatically and even to reduce them at times. For many European borderlands, this was a remarkable transition from enemies to partners. There are now more opportunities than at any time before for people to make up their own minds about how they feel about their neighbors. While this rarely results in shared identities, it contributes to the development of a sense of "cultural pragmatism" that can help advance border bridging.

The Institutional and Governance Dimension

Traditionally there were no permanent institutions that crossed European borders. The state territorial-administrative organization gravitated toward national capitals, and state borders formed the territorial limits of national institutions and their administrative jurisdictions, separating different systems of political organization. Cross-border contacts, when they existed at all, were largely routed through national institutions. Euroregions have changed this situation. They constitute new institutional frameworks of territorial governance beyond the scope of traditional national institutions (Perkmann 2002, 2003). Although the latter are part of the multilevel networks that define the governance of Euroregions, there are no national institutions that have jurisdiction over the entire territory of a Euroregion. The administrative bodies of Euroregions, such as presidencies, secretariats, and commissions, are not national but cross-border in nature.

The extent to which cross-border governance institutions can act as autonomous cross-border structures has been a matter of intense debate (Kramsch 2002b; Perkmann 2007a, 2007b). While the governance of Euroregions represents a departure from the hierarchical model of government, cross-border institutions are generally weak and lack key decision-making powers that continue to rest with national and supranational actors. At the same time, they often display a reduced degree of cross-border integration, as it is not uncommon that each borderland has its own set of institutions mirroring each other across the border. Although these institutions do work together across borders, their logic remains national in essence (Fall 2005).

One of the most important issues that beleaguered cross-border governance from the beginning was the lack of mechanisms for allowing public representation (Kramsch 2001; O'Dowd 2002a). There are no cross-border elections to choose representatives for Euroregion governance bodies, and in many cases the personnel staffing cross-border institutions are selected from the employees of the local administrations functioning in the borderlands. This void has created a "democratic deficit" in Euroregions that causes their governance to be dominated by technocratic institutions with limited capacity for generating their own cross-border political agency. In the few cases where bottom-up political agency has materialized, the governance networks rely predominantly on cross-border interpersonal relationships between local leaders than on the structural steadiness of cross-border institutions. This overreliance on interpersonal relations in the governance process as a substitute for the lack of formal institutional power has often affected the consistency of border-bridging processes. As local leaders in the borderlands can change following national elections, the intensity of cross-border cooperation can experience ups and downs as well.

On the other hand, cross-border governance has made major contributions to border bridging by assuring a measure of stability and structure to cross-border cooperation practices, as well as by incorporating local actors into cross-border decision making. Today, the vast majority of local administrations in Europe's borderlands include in their development strategies some form of cross-border cooperation plans, even if they do not actively pursue them. In other words, the cross-border cooperation paradigm has become routine border-bridging policy. Moreover, the implementation of EU initiatives such as the EGTC presents additional potential for strengthening cross-border institutions by increasing their decision-making powers and making them more representative of the needs and aspirations of civil society.

The dimensions of border change discussed here reveal that border-bridging does take place but not in the way it was initially anticipated. When analyzing cross-border cooperation in Euroregions, we need to keep in mind the starting point and the context in which it occurred. The internal borderlands of the European Union have transitioned from a situation of separation to a process of integration. For the most part this has been a top-down enterprise that has not penetrated deep enough into civil society to allow the emergence of autonomous cross-border spaces of living. However, the existence of cross-border legal frameworks, institutions, and territories represents a concrete departure from the previous situation and holds significant potential for further border bridging. This suggests that the achievements and failures of cross-border cooperation have to be made sense of from the perspective of a long-term process that cannot produce the same outcomes in all contexts.

Conclusion

We are living in a period of border change with profound impacts on social life. Given that border making constitutes a key principle for organizing social relations in space, when borders change functions, shapes, and meanings, people's lives change as well. This is all the more important to realize if we consider that border making is essentially an act of power. Border-making power is power over people's lives. Thus, understanding borders can aid us in recognizing these power relations and enable us to act in a way that maximizes our rights and improves social justice and therefore the quality of our lives. The primary goal of this book has been to examine border making by describing its underlying causes and discussing its impact on society. This volume does not constitute a complete or definitive explanation of borders, as they are contextual and multifaceted phenomena that resist exhaustive explanations. Instead this book has put forward a road map to assist in navigating the multiple facets of border making. This road map has included a series of major points of reference, grounded in a spatial perspective, to guide the reader in interpreting the relationship between borders and society.

Central to this book has been the social construction of borders. The view adopted here is that borders are human made and are not naturally occurring divisions between people and places. The difference that borders mark does not have a fixed, preexisting meaning. It is humans who interpret difference and define what it means, for whom, at what times, and in what places. Humans set the threshold of tolerance for difference that ultimately results in borders. We have used border making for a long time as a power strategy for ordering society and space according to our belief systems. As a consequence, border making has been rooted in the cultural practices of a society. This rootedness has produced borders that are inherently unfinished, flexible, and changing.

Emphasis on the social construction of borders has shifted the focus from the product to the process. This is to say that understanding the processes that lead to the erection of borders (i.e., who makes borders, why, and how they acquire their shape) reveals more about the nature of borders than determining the course they follow or the shape they assume at one time or another (i.e., how borders have changed location and what borders look like). The point here is that the product is the outcome of the process. Twenty-first-century state borders have to be understood in relation to the processes and circumstances that produce them. Where and what kinds of borders exist depends on why and how borders are built.

Another major aspect brought to the fore by the social constructionist perspective has been the dialectical nature of borders. Borders epitomize contradictory forces—such as separation and contact or inclusion and exclusion—that take on a variety of meanings and perform a variety of functions simultaneously. This multifaceted nature has made border making a tricky business. Whenever governments have chosen to restrict cross-border movement, for example, the forces responsible for this phenomenon have reacted by pushing back for more cross-border movement. The result has been that borders have always had various degrees of permeability. They have performed regulatory roles with regard to interaction in space rather than strictly containing it. In this light, the current battle over the making of twenty-first-century state borders appears to be less about opening or closing them and more about defining the meaning and the scope of their permeability.

In space, border permeability has assumed various geographies. The territorial appearance of state borders has changed frequently since antiquity to reflect how societies imagined difference and space. Early states had frontiers that provided a gradual territorial transition to their neighbors. They were the result of a mode of organization of social relations that relied on authority over subjects to assert authority over territory. The advent of the Enlightenment in eighteenth-century Europe, with its belief that the world can be rationally understood by rigorously dividing it into meaningful categories, left little conceptual room for the ambiguity characteristic of frontiers. By the early twentieth century, frontiers were replaced by sharp border lines that provided abrupt territorial transitions from one state to another and a clear differentiation between a state's inside and its outside. The borders of the state and of society were assumed to overlap, and authority over territory was used to assert authority over subjects. At the same time, the ideologies of nationalism and capitalism helped to consolidate border lines as default divisions between states, while colonialism helped to globalize this particular border geography by exporting it from Europe to the rest of the world. Borders continued to remain permeable, but their meaning changed and movement across them became more controlled.

In the late twentieth century, state border lines came under steady pressure from various globalization processes whose logic of movement required increased permeability. Different aspects of social life such as economic exchanges, management of the environment, human rights regimes, organized crime, and others developed patterns of spatial organization that cut through state borders. These developments led to a growing disconnection between the geography of globalization flows and the ability of border lines to regulate it. In turn, this rendered problematic the assumption that borders function as walls for containing social relations inside a state's territories and for providing meaningful differentiation between inside and outside a state's realms.

One notable outcome of globalization has been the emergence of a major twenty-first-century paradox that has found expression in the desire to cross all borders while at the same time desiring to erect borders of all kinds and shapes. This paradox has invited considerable border-making tension between simultaneous demands for unimpeded cross-border mobility on the one hand and for reliable territorial security on the other. In response to this situation, borders have undergone a multifaceted process of change aimed at readjusting their permeability to meet the demands of new globalization realities. The main objective has been to achieve a regime of highly selective permeability that can allow the free flow of exchanges that powerful border-making stakeholders consider desirable, while also blocking the flow of exchanges that these stakeholders consider undesirable. This dual capacity, however, implied thorough control over cross-border movement that border lines alone were not able to deliver given their territorial rigidity. In order to implement such a border regime, the change had to include not only the redefinition of border functions but the redefinition of their geography as well. In other words, borders had to take on additional territorial configurations to become articulate and mobile.

To make better sense of how and what kind of new border spaces are being produced, it is useful to think in terms of de- and reterritorialization and de- and rebordering dynamics. While some border lines in some places are dismantled or have their barrier functions significantly diminished, other borders in other places are erected. These new borders often do not maintain a linear appearance and are not located at the margins of a state's territory. Three main types of border spaces can be associated with globalization's current political, economic, and cultural geographies—borderlands, networked borders, and border lines. In the first case, the territorial depth of borders is acknowledged and is managed as a transitional space that connects state territories. In the second case, borders acquire territorial mobility by being embedded into flows so that bordering can be performed anyplace on Earth. In the last case, borders preserve the appeal of sharp lines and become reinforced by fences and walls. The result of these restructuring dynamics is the multiplication of borders, the diversification of their territorial shape, and the diffusion of borders inside state territories. Globalization, despite being commonly associated with a "borderless world," has in fact produced more rather than fewer borders and has increased rather than decreased their complexity.

At the beginning of the twenty-first century, security concerns regarding the control of mobility constitute the main driving force behind border making. If we consider that the bordering of the twentieth century was about securing state territories, then the bordering of the twenty-first century appears to be about securing mobility. In recent years, there has been a constant retreat of traditional border regulatory functions in matters concerning economic and social protection, and a significant increase of focus on the most basic functions such as the provision of security. Efforts to settle globalization's border paradox through selective permeability, while at the same time preserving the territorial state as the exclusive form of political organization in the world, create the perception of an intrinsic conflict between security and mobility. Various transnational flows, from immigration and trade to terrorism and organized crime, are frequently lumped together in public discourse and are presented as potential "threats" to the existence of a society as well as to the personal livelihoods of its citizens.

In this worldview, borders are seen as sites and tools for securitizing global flows. The belief is that risk management strategies can be employed at the border to predict risks by meaningfully differentiating between "good" and "bad" mobility. The human body has become the preferred target of these strategies which work under the assumption that identifying bodies is similar to knowing the identities of the people they belong to. To this end, we are in the midst of a rush to embed borders into the body in order to achieve control of mobility at the smallest spatial scale. The body itself has become the border, a very personal one that can be continually monitored with the help of technology as the body moves through space. Technology is the linchpin of the new bordering practices. A vast array of digital information technologies work as an interface for integrating embodied borders and risk assessment systems to automate risk prediction and ultimately border crossing. Consequently, these technologies are entrusted with key decision-making powers about people's lives. Biometric technology, used to digitize bodily data such as fingerprints and iris patterns in order to store them in passport chips and border security–related databases, is one such example. RFID technology, used to broadcast these bodily data wirelessly so that their owners' movement can be tracked without being stopped at the border, is another example.

Border securitization practices raise major concerns about their efficiency as well as about their costs in terms of democratic freedoms. In this book I have sought to challenge the dominant assumption underlying the logic of movement control in the twenty-first century that increased control of society is an inevitable side effect of globalization and a small price to pay for social and personal security. Twenty-first-century borders are incorporated into the fabric of societies where people encounter them regularly during their daily activities, often without being aware of their presence. People's identities are routinely screened before they even reach the state border, while vast amounts of data about their lives are surreptitiously collected by border enforcement agencies and stored in databases people cannot control. Moreover, substantial border-making authority is transferred from state institutions that are accountable to the public to private institutions that are accountable to a restricted number of citizens with specific interests. Despite these costs, there is little to prove that these mass surveillance practices have significantly improved societal or personal security. Terrorist attacks have continued across the world, immigration flows show few signs of letting up, and the adverse effects of unregulated global economic flows continue to widen the gap between the rich and the poor inside as well as between countries. On the other hand, control over the daily lives of individuals has deepened. Control has become more politicized and more reliant on faceless technologies that cannot be held accountable in a court of law. The sources of control have multiplied and have become diffused in society, making it more difficult to identify the controllers, thus further shedding responsibility for control. These developments are weakening the prospects for democratic life while failing to improve the quality of life in society. They call for a reassessment of border securitization practices to make sure they are not doing more to oppress societies than to protect them.

Border bridging is another major force driving contemporary border making. During the last two decades, cross-border cooperation has become the leading border-bridging process and an established governance practice. It has made major contributions to increasing border permeability by providing a framework that enables direct interaction across borders. Much of the activity is concentrated in the borderlands' neighboring border lines and includes sub-, supra-, and transnational actors. Cross-border cooperation has significant impacts on border reterritorialization, as it can lead to the formation of cross-border regions where social life can be organized across border lines to better reflect local needs. Nonetheless, cross-border cooperation is an uneven process that produces different outcomes in different regional contexts. Despite its vast border-bridging potential, it has fallen short of expectations for integrating neighboring borderlands at the local level. In many instances, cross-border cooperation is used as a glocal strategy to position national borderlands to make them attractive destinations for global economic flows. In other instances, bottom-up integration in cross-border regions is resisted at the national level because it is perceived as being in conflict with the demands of state territorial sovereignty. Although these shortcomings have detrimental effects on border bridging, cross-border cooperation practices are actively working to transform borders and to bring about new border spaces. Their overall impact is to unsettle the meaning of state borders as unequivocal division lines and to accommodate increased cross-border mobility.

The exploration of border spaces in this book has pointed out the central place border-making power occupies in the ordering of our lives. In a time of increasing pressure for this ordering to become more thorough and personal, and when technology offers unparalleled capabilities for achieving this end, it is only by being aware of the ways in which border making affects us that we can have a say over how this power should be used and to what ends in order to achieve positive change in our lives.

References

Aas, K. F. 2006. The Body Does Not Lie: Identity, Risk and Trust in Technoculture. *Crime, Media, Culture* 2:143–158.

Ackleson, J. 2005a. Constructing Security on the U.S.-Mexico Border. *Political Geography* 24 (2): 164–184.

———. 2005b. Border Security in Risk Society. *Journal of Borderlands Studies* 20 (1): 1–22.

Agamben, G. 1998. *Homo Sacer: Sovereign Power and Bare Life*. Stanford, CA: Stanford University Press.

———. 2005. *State of Exception*. Chicago: University of Chicago Press.

Agnew, J. 1994. The Territorial Trap: The Geographical Assumptions of International Relations Theory. *Review of International Political Economy* 1 (1): 53–80.

———. 1998. *Geopolitics: Re-Visioning World Politics*. London: Routledge.

———. 2002. The "Civilisational" Roots of European National Boundaries. In D. Kaplan and I. Hakli, eds., *Boundaries and Place*. Lanham, MD: Rowman & Littlefield. Pp. 18–33.

———. 2007. No Borders, No Nations: Making Greece in Macedonia. *Annals of the Association of American Geographers* 97 (2): 398–422.

———. 2009. *Globalization and Sovereignty*. Lanham, MD: Rowman & Littlefield.

Albert, M. 1998. On Boundaries, Territory and Postmodernity: An International Relations Perspective. *Geopolitics* 3 (1): 53–68.

Albert, M., Jacobson, D., and Lapid, Y., eds. 2001. *Identities, Orders, Borders: Rethinking International Relations Theory*. Minneapolis: University of Minnesota Press.

Albrecht, K. 2008. RFID Tag—You're It. *Scientific American*, September.

Ali, S. H., and Keil, R. 2006. Global Cities and the Spread of Infectious Disease: The Case of Severe Acute Respiratory Syndrome (SARS) in Toronto, Canada. *Urban Studies* 43:491–509.

Allen, J., Massey, D., and Cochrane, A. 1998. *Rethinking the Region.* New York: Routledge.

Alper, D. 1996. The Idea of Cascadia: Emergent Regionalisms in the Pacific Northwest-Western Canada. *Journal of Borderland Studies* 11 (2): 1–22.

Amilhat-Szary, A.-L. 2003. L'intégration Continentale aux Marges du MERCOSUR: les échelles d'un Processus Transfrontalier et Transandin. *Revue de Géographie Alpine* 91 (3): 47–56.

———. 2007. Are Borders More Easily Crossed Today? The Paradox of Contemporary Trans-Border Mobility in the Andes. *Geopolitics* 12:1-18.

Amilhat-Szary, A.-L., and Fourny, M.-C., eds. 2006. *Après les Frontières, avec la Frontière: Nouvelles Dynamiques Transfrontalières en Europe.* La Tour d'Aigues: Éditions de l'Aube.

Amoore, L. 2006. Biometric Borders: Governing Mobilities in the War on Terror. *Political Geography* 25:336–351.

———. 2009. Algorithmic War: Everyday Geographies of the War on Terror. *Antipode* 41:49–69.

Amoore, L., and de Goede, M. 2008. Governing by Risk in the War on Terror. In L. Amoore and M. de Goede, eds., *Risk and the War on Terror.* London: Routledge. Pp. 5–19.

Ancel, J. 1938. *Géographie des Frontières.* Paris: Gallimard.

Anderson, B. 1991. *Imagined Communities: Reflections on the Origin and Spread of Nationalism.* London: Verso.

Anderson, J. 1996. The Shifting Stage of Politics: New Medieval and Postmodern Territorialities. *Environment and Planning D* 14 (2): 133–155.

Anderson, J., and O'Dowd, L. 1999. Borders, Border Regions and Territoriality: Contradictory Meanings, Changing Significance. *Regional Studies* 33 (7): 593–604.

Anderson, J., O'Dowd, L., and Wilson, T. M. 2003. Why Study Borders Now? In J. Anderson, L. O'Dowd, and T. M. Wilson, eds., *New Borders for a Changing Europe.* London: Frank Cass. Pp. 1–12.

Anderson, M. 1996. *Frontiers: Territory and State Formation in the Modern World.* Cambridge: Polity Press.

Anderson, M., and Bort, E. 2001. *The Frontiers of the European Union.* Houndmills: Palgrave.

Andreas, P. 2000. *Border Games: Policing the U.S.-Mexico Divide.* Ithaca, NY: Cornell University Press.

———. 2003. A Tale of Two Borders: The U.S.-Canada and U.S.-Mexico Lines after 9–11. In P. Andreas and T. J. Biersteker, eds., *The Rebordering of North America.* New York: Routledge. Pp. 11–23.

Andreas, P., and Biersteker, T. J., eds. 2003. *The Rebordering of North America: Integration and Exclusion in a New Security Context.* New York: Routledge.

Angel, D. P., Hamilton, T., and Huber, M. T. 2007. Global Environmental Standards for Industry. *Annual Review of Environment and Resources* 32:295–316.

Ansell, C., and Di Palma, G., eds. 2004. *Restructuring Territoriality: Europe and the United States Compared.* Cambridge: Cambridge University Press.

Apap, J., and Tchorbadjiyska, A. 2004. What about the Neighbours? The Impact of Schengen along the EU's External Borders. *Centre for European Policy Stud-*

ies, Working Document No. 210. Available at http://shop.ceps.be/BookDetail .php?item_id=1171.

Appadurai, A. 1996. *Modernity at Large: Cultural Dimensions of Globalization.* Minneapolis: University of Minnesota Press.

Aradau, C., and van Munster, R. 2007. Governing Terrorism through Risk: Taking Precautions, (Un)Knowing the Future. *European Journal of International Relations* 13 (1): 89–115.

Arbaret-Schulz, C., Beyer, A., Permay, J., Reitel, B., Selimanovski, C., Sohn, C., and Zander P. 2004. La frontière, un objet spatial en mutation. EspacesTemps.net . Available at http://espacestemps.net/document842.html.

Arieli, T. 2010. National and Regional Governance of the Israel-Jordan Border Region. Paper presented at the conference Borders, Territory and Conflict in a Globalizing World, Beersheba, Israel, July 6–11.

Axford, B. 2006. The Dialectic of Networks and Borders in Europe: Reviewing Topological Presuppositions. *Comparative European Politics* 4/3:160–182.

Baker, S. 1996. Punctured Sovereignty, Border Regions and the Environment within the European Union. In L. O'Dowd and T. M. Wilson, eds., *Borders, Nations and States.* Avebury: Aldershot. Pp. 19–50.

Baldaccini, A. 2008. Counter-Terrorism and the EU Strategy for Border Security: Framing Suspects with Biometric Documents and Databases. *European Journal of Migration and Law* 10 (1): 31–49.

Balibar, E. 2002. *Politics and the Other Scene.* London: Verso.

———. 2004. *We, the People of Europe? Reflections on Transnational Citizenship.* Princeton, NJ: Princeton University Press.

Bank for International Settlements. 2010. *Triennial Central Bank Survey of Foreign Exchange and Derivatives Market Activity in 2010.* Basel, Switzerland. Available at http://www.bis.org/publ/rpfxf10t.pdf.

Batt, J. 2003. The Enlarged EU's External Borders—The Regional Dimension. In J. Batt, D. Lynch, A. Missiroli, M. Ortega, and D. Triantaphyllou, *Partners and Neighbors: A CFSP for a Wider Europe.* Paris: EU Institute for Security Studies 64:102–118.

Bauman, Z. 1998. *Globalization: The Human Consequences.* Cambridge: Polity Press.

Beck, U. 1998. Politics of Risk Society. In J. Franklin, ed., *The Politics of Risk Society.* Cambridge: Polity Press. Pp. 9–22.

Bednarz, D., Follath, E. Schult, C., Smoltczyk, A., Stark, H., and Zand, B. 2010. Targeted Killing in Dubai: A Mossad Operation Gone Awry? *Der Spiegel*, February 23.

Berg, E., and Ehin, P. 2006. What Kind of Border Regime is in the Making? Towards a Differentiated and Uneven Border Strategy. *Cooperation and Conflict* 41 (1): 53–71.

Berg, E., and van Houtum, H., eds. 2003. *Routing Borders between Territories, Discourses and Practices.* Aldershot: Ashgate.

Bernstein, N. 2009. U.S. to Reform Policy on Detention for Immigrants. *New York Times*, August 6.

Bigo, D. 2001. The Möbius Ribbon of Security(ies). In M. Albert, D. Jacobson, and Y. Lapid, eds., *Identities, Borders, Orders.* Minneapolis: University of Minnesota Press. Pp. 91–116.

Blake, G. H. 1992. International Boundaries and Territorial Stability in the Middle East: An Assessment. *GeoJournal* 28 (3): 365–376.

Blatter, J. 2001. Debordering the World of States: Towards a Multi-Level System in Europe and a Multi-Polity System in North America? *European Journal of International Relations* 7 (2): 175–210.

———. 2003. Beyond Hierarchies and Networks: Institutional Logics and Change in Transboundary Spaces. *Governance* 16 (4): 503–526.

Boid, D. 2010. Social Network Sites as Networked Publics: Affordances, Dynamics, and Implications. In Z. Papacharissi, ed., *A Networked Self*. New York: Routledge. Pp. 39–58.

Brenner, N. 1999a. Beyond State-centrism? Space, Territory, and Geographical Scale in Globalization Studies. *Theory and Society* 28:39–78.

———. 1999b. Globalisation as Reterritorialisation: The Re-scaling of Urban Governance in the European Union. *Urban Studies* 36 (3): 431–451.

Brenner, N., Jessop, B., Jones, M., and Macleod, G. 2003. Introduction: State Space in Question. In N. Brenner, B. Jessop, M. Jones, and G. Macleod, eds., *State/Space*. Oxford: Blackwell Publishing. Pp. 1–26.

Brothers, C. 2008. E.U. Passes Tough Migrant Measure. *New York Times*, June 19.

Brunet-Jailly, E. 2007. Border Security and Porosity: An Introduction. In E. Brunet-Jailly, ed., *Borderlands: Comparing Border Security in North America and Europe*. Ottawa: University of Ottawa Press. Pp. 1–18.

Bruslé, L. P. 2007. The Front and the Line: The Paradox of South American Frontiers Applied to the Bolivian Case. *Geopolitics* 12:57–77.

Bucken-Knapp, G., and Schack, M. 2001. Borders Matter, but How? In G. Bucken-Knapp and M. Schack, eds., *Borders Matter*. Aabenraa: IFG. Pp. 13–29.

Bukowski, J., Piattoni, S., and Smyrl, M., eds. 2003. *Between Europeanization and Local Societies: The Space for Territorial Governance*. Lanham, MD: Rowman & Littlefield.

Buzan, B. 1993. Societal Security, State Security and Internationalization. In O. Waever, B. Buzan, M. Kelstrup, and P. Lemaitre, eds., *Identity, Migration and the New Security Agenda in Europe*. London: Pinter. Pp. 41–58.

Byers, M. 2000. The Law and Politics of the Pinochet Case. *Duke Journal of Comparative and International Law* 10:415–441.

Camilleri, M. T. 2004. The Challenges of Sovereign Borders in the Post–Cold War Era's Refugees and Humanitarian Crises. In H. Hensel, ed., *Sovereignty and the Global Community*. Aldershot: Ashgate. Pp. 83–104.

Castells, M. 2000. *The Rise of the Network Society*. Oxford: Blackwell.

Christiansen, T., and Jorgenson, K. E. 2000. Transnational Governance "Above" and "Below" the State: The Changing Nature of Borders in the New Europe. *Regional and Federal Studies* 10 (2): 62–77.

Clement, N., Ganster, P., and Sweedler, A. 1999. Development, Environment, and Security in Asymmetrical Border Regions: European and North American Perspectives. In H. Eskelinen, I. Liikanen, and J. Oksa, eds., *Curtains of Iron and Gold*. Aldershot: Ashgate. Pp. 243–284.

Coleman, M. 2005. US Statecraft and the US-Mexico Border as Security/Economy Nexus. *Political Geography* 24 (2): 185–209.

———. 2007a. A Geopolitics of Engagement: Neoliberalism and the War on Terrorism at the Mexico-US Border. *Geopolitics* 12 (4): 607–634.

———. 2007b. Immigration Geopolitics beyond the Mexico-US Border. *Antipode* 38 (1): 54–76.

Collyer, M. 2008. Mediterranean Migration Management or the Externalisation of EU Policy? In Y. Zoubir and H. Amirah-Fernandez, eds., *Contemporary North Africa*. London: Routledge. Pp. 159–178.

Commission of the European Communities. 2003. *Wider Europe—Neighbourhood: A New Framework for Relations with Our Eastern and Southern Neighbours.* Brussels, November 3. Available at http://europa.eu.int/comm/world/enp/index_en.htm.

Conversi, D. 1999. Nationalism, Boundaries, and Violence. *Millennium* 28:553–584.

Cox, K. 2002. *Political Geography: Territory, State and Society*. Malden, MA: Blackwell.

Cresswell, T. 2010. Towards a Politics of Mobility. *Environment and Planning D* 28:17–31.

Dalby, S. 1998. Globalization or Global Apartheid? Boundaries and Knowledge in Postmodern Times. *Geopolitics* 3 (1): 132–150.

Dalin, C. 1984/2005. The Great Wall of China. In P. Ganster and D. Lorey, eds., *Borders and Border Politics in a Globalizing World*. Lanham, MD: SR Books. Pp. 11–20.

Davidson, D., and Kim, G. 2009. Additional Powers of Search and Seizure at and near the Border. *Border Policy Brief* 4 (3): 1–4.

Delanty, G. 2006. Borders in a Changing Europe: Dynamics of Openness and Closure. *Comparative European Politics* 4:183–202.

de Larrinaga, M., and Doucet, M. 2008. Sovereign Power and the Biopolitics of Human Security. *Security Dialogue* 39 (5): 517–537.

Deleuze, G., and Guattari, F. 1977. *Anti-Oedipus: Capitalism and Schizophrenia*. Minneapolis: University of Minnesota Press.

Delli Zotti, G. 1996. Transfrontier Co-operation at the External Borders of the EU: Implications for Sovereignty. In L. O'Dowd and T. M. Wilson, eds., *Borders, Nations and States*. Aldershot: Avebury. Pp. 51–72.

Department of Homeland Security. 2006. *Privacy Impact Assessment for the Automated Targeting System*. November 22.

———. 2008. *Privacy Impact Assessment for the Use of Radio Frequency Identification (RFID) Technology for Border Crossings*. January 22.

Dicken, P., Kelly, P. F., Olds, K., and Yeung, H. W.-C. 2001. Chains and Networks, Territories and Scales: Towards a Relational Framework for Analysing the Global Economy. *Global Networks* 1 (2): 89–112.

Diener, A., and Hagen, J. 2009. Theorizing Borders in a "Borderless World": Globalization, Territory and Identity. *Geography Compass* 3 (3): 1196–1216.

Dillon, M. 2007. Governing through Contingency: The Security of Biopolitical Governance. *Political Geography* 26 (1): 41–47.

Dillon, M., and Lobo-Guerrero, L. 2008. Biopolitics of Security in the 21st Century: An Introduction. *Review of International Studies* 34:265–292.

Dobson, J., and Fisher, P. 2007. The Panopticon's Changing Geography. *Geographical Review* 97:307–323.

Dodds, K. 2008. Icy Geopolitics. *Environment and Planning D* 26:1–6.

Donnan, H., and Wilson, T. 1999. *Borders: Frontiers of Identity, Nation and State.* Oxford: Berg.

———. 2003. Territoriality, Anthropology and the Interstitial: Subversion and Support in European Borderlands. *European Journal of Anthropology* 41 (3): 9–25.

Duchacek, I. 1986. International Competence of Subnational Governments: Borderlands and Beyond. In O. J. Martinez, ed., *Across Boundaries*. El Paso: Texan Western Press. Pp. 11–30.

Dupeyron, B. 2009. Perspectives on Mercosur Borders and Border Spaces: Implications for Border Theories. *Journal of Borderlands Studies* 24 (3): 59–68.

Eskelinen, H., Liikanen, I., and Oksa, J., eds. 1999. *Curtains of Iron and Gold: Reconstructing Borders and Scales of Interaction*. Aldershot: Ashgate.

Elden, S. 2005a. Missing the Point: Globalization, Deterritorialization and the Space of the World. *Transactions of the Institute of British Geographers* 30:8–19.

———. 2005b. Territorial Integrity and the War on Terror. *Environment and Planning A* 37:2083–2104.

———. 2007a. Terror and Territory. *Antipode* 39:821–845.

———. 2007b. Governmentality, Calculation, Territory. *Environment and Planning D* 25:562–580.

Epstein, C. 2007. Guilty Bodies, Productive Bodies, Destructive Bodies: Crossing the Biometric Borders. *International Political Sociology* 1 (2): 149–164.

———. 2008. Embodying Risk: Using Biometrics to Protect the Borders. In L. Amoore and M. de Goede, eds., *Risk and the War on Terror*. London: Routledge. Pp. 178–193.

Eriksson, J., and Giacomello, G. 2009. Who Controls the Internet? Beyond the Obstinacy or Obsolescence of the State. *International Studies Review* 11 (1): 205–230.

Falah, G.-W., Flint, C., and Mamadouh, V. 2006. Just War and Extraterritoriality: The Popular Geopolitics of the United States' War on Iraq as Reflected in Newspapers of the Arab World. *Annals of the Association of American Geographers* 96:142–164.

Fall, J. 2005. *Drawing the Line: Nature, Hybridity and Politics in Transboundary Spaces*. Aldershot: Ashgate.

Fawcett, C. 1918. *Frontiers: A Study in Political Geography*. Oxford: Oxford University Press.

Ferrer-Gallardo, X. 2008. The Spanish–Moroccan Border Complex: Processes of Geopolitical, Functional and Symbolic Rebordering. *Political Geography* 27 (3): 301–321.

Ferrera, M. 2004. Social Citizenship in the European Union: Toward a Spatial Reconfiguration? In C. Ansell and G. Di Palma, eds., *Restructuring Territoriality*. Cambridge: Cambridge University Press. Pp. 90–121.

Fidler, D. P. 2003. SARS: Political Pathology of the First Post-Westphalian Pathogen. *The Journal of Law, Medicine & Ethics* 31 (4): 485–505.

Forsberg, T., ed. 1995. *Contested Territories: Border Disputes on the Edge of the Former Soviet Empire*. London: Edward Elgar.

Foucault, M. 1977. *Discipline and Punish: The Birth of the Prison*. London: Penguin.

———. 1978. *The History of Sexuality: An Introduction*. New York: Vintage.

———. 2007. *Security, Territory, Population: Lectures at the College de France, 1977–1978.* New York: Palgrave Macmillan.

———. 2008. *The Birth of Biopolitics: Lectures at the College de France, 1978–1979.* New York: Palgrave Macmillan.

Foucher, M. 1991. *Fronts et Frontières: Un Tour du Monde Géopolitique.* Paris: Fayard.

———. 2007. *L'Obsession des Frontières.* Paris: Perrin.

Fuller, T., Conde, C., Fugal, J., and Ng, C. 2008. The Melamine Stain: One Sign of a Worldwide Problem. *New York Times,* October 12.

Ganster, P., and Lorey, D. E., eds. 2005. *Borders and Border Politics in a Globalizing World.* Lanham, MD: SR Books.

Giddens, A. 1987. *The Nation-State and Violence.* London: Polity Press.

Gottmann, J. 1973. *The Significance of Territory.* Charlottesville: University of Virginia Press.

Goyon, J.-K. 1993. Égypte Pharaonique: Le Roi Frontière. *Travaux de la Maison de l'Orient* 21:9–14.

Green, P. 2006. State Crime beyond Borders: Europe and the Outsourcing of Irregular Migration Control. In S. Pickering and L. Weber, eds., *Borders, Mobility and Technologies of Control.* Dordrecht: Springer. Pp. 196–166.

Gregory, D. 2004. The Angel of Iraq. *Environment and Planning D* 22:317–324.

———. 2006. The Black Flag: Guantanamo Bay and the Space of Exception. *Geografiska Annaler B* 88 (4): 405–427.

———. 2007. Vanishing Points: Law, Violence, and Exception in the Global War Prison. In D. Gregory and A. Pred, eds., *Violent Geographies.* New York: Routledge. Pp. 205–235.

Grosby, S. 1995. Territoriality: The Transcendental, Primordial Feature of Modern Societies. *Nations and Nationalism* 1 (2): 143–162.

Grundy-Warr, C. 2002. Cross-Border Regionalism through a "South-East Asian" Looking-Glass. *Space & Polity* 6 (2): 215–225.

Guild, E., Carrera, S., and Geyer, F. 2008. The Commission's New Border Package: Does It Take Us One Step Closer to a "Cyber-Fortress Europe"? *Centre for European Policy Studies,* policy brief, 154:1–5. Available at http://www.ceps.eu/node/1342.

Hakli, I., and Kaplan, D. 2002. Learning from Europe? Borderlands in Social and Geographical Context. In D. Kaplan and I. Hakli, eds., *Boundaries and Place.* Lanham, MD: Rowman & Littlefield. Pp. 1–17.

Hartshorne, R. 1936. Suggestions on the Terminology of Political Boundaries. *Annals of the Association of American Geographers* 26 (1): 56–57.

Harvey, D. 1989. *The Condition of Postmodernity.* Oxford: Basil Blackwell.

———. 2000. *Spaces of Hope.* Berkley: University of California Press.

Harvie, C. 1994. *The Rise of Regional Europe.* London: Routledge.

Heffernan, M. 1998. *The Meaning of Europe: Geography and Geopolitics.* London: Arnold.

Hegg, S., and Ossenbrugge, J. 2002. State Formation and Territoriality in the European Union. *Geopolitics* 7 (3): 75–88.

Herbst, J. 1989. The Creation and Maintenance of National Boundaries in Africa. *International Organization* 43 (4): 673–692.

Heussner, K. M. 2009. Surgically Altered Fingerprints Help Woman Evade Immigration. ABC News, December 11. Available at http://abcnews.go.com/Technology/GadgetGuide/surgically-altered-fingerprints-woman-evade-immigration/story?id=9302505&page=3.

Hevilla, C., and Zusman, P. 2009. Borders Which Unite and Disunite: Mobilities and Development of New Territorialities on the Chile-Argentina Frontier. *Journal of Borderlands Studies* 24 (3): 83–96.

Hoepman, J. H., Hubbers, E., Jacobs, B., Oostdijk, M., and Schreur, R. W. 2006. Crossing Borders: Security and Privacy Issues of the European e-Passport. In H. Yoshiura, K. Sakurai, K. Rannenberg, Y. Murayama, and S. Kawamura, eds., *International Workshop on Security, Lecture Notes in Computer Science* 4266. Berlin: Springer. Pp. 152–167.

Huysmans, J. 2006. *The Politics of Insecurity: Fear, Migration and Asylum in the EU.* London: Routledge.

Hyndman, J. 2007. Conflict, Citizenship, and Human Security: Geographies of Protection. In D. Cohen and E. Gilbert, eds., *War, Citizenship, Territory.* New York: Routledge. Pp. 241–257.

Hyndman, J., and Mountz, A. 2007. Refuge or Refusal: Geography of Exclusion. In D. Gregory and A. Pred, eds., *Violent Geographies.* New York: Routledge. Pp. 77–92.

———. 2008. Another Brick in the Wall? Neo-refoulement and the Externalisation of Asylum in Europe and Australia. *Government & Opposition* 43 (2): 249–269.

International Criminal Court. 2008. *Outreach Report.* ICC-CPI-20081120-PR375. Available at http://www.icc-cpi.int/NR/rdonlyres/AE9B69EB-2692-4F9C-8F08-B3844FE397C7/279073/Outreach_report2008enLR.pdf.

International Labour Organization. 2008. *Message by Juan Somavia Director-General of the International Labour Office on the Occasion of International Migrants Day.* December 18. Available at: http://www.ilo.org/public/english/bureau/dgo/speeches/somavia/2008/migrants.pdf.

Jessop B. 2002. The Political Economy of Scale. In M. Perkmann and N. L. Sum, eds., *Globalisation, Regionalisation and Cross-Border Regions.* London: Palgrave. Pp. 25–49.

Jones, R. 2009a. Agents of Exception: Border Security and the Marginalization of Muslims in India. *Environment and Planning D* 27:879–897.

———. 2009b. Geopolitical Boundary Narratives, the Global War on Terror and Border Fencing in India. *Transactions of the Institute of British Geographers* 34:290–304.

Jones, S. B. 1945. *Boundary-Making: A Handbook for Statesmen, Treaty Editors and Boundary Commissioners.* Washington, DC: Carnegie Endowment.

Jonsson, C., Tagil, S., and Tornqvist, G. 2000. *Organizing European Space.* London: SAGE.

Juels, A. 2006. RFID Security and Privacy: A Research Survey. *IEEE Journal on Selected Areas in Communications* 24 (2): 381–394.

Kaplan, D., and Hakli, I., eds. 2002. *Boundaries and Place: European Borderlands in Geographical Context.* Lanham, MD: Rowman & Littlefield.

Kazancigil, A., ed. 1986. *The State in Global Perspective.* Dorset: Blackmore Press.

Kearney, M. 1991. Borders and Boundaries of State and Self at the End of Empire. *Journal of Historical Sociology* 4 (1): 52–74.

Keating, M. 1995. Europeanism and Regionalism. In B. Jones and M. Keating, eds., *The European Union and the Regions*. Clarendon: Oxford. Pp. 1–22.

———. 1998. *The New Regionalism in Western Europe*. Cheltenham: Edward Elgar.

Kepka, J., and Murphy, A. 2002. Euroregions in Comparative Perspective. In D. Kaplan and I. Hakli, eds., *Boundaries and Place*. Lanham, MD: Rowman & Littlefield. Pp. 50–70.

Knight, D. 1982. Identity and Territory: Geographical Perspectives on Nationalism and Regionalism. *Annals of the Association of American Geographers* 72:514–531.

Knippenberg, H., and Markusse, J., eds. 1999. *Nationalising and Denationalising European Border Regions, 1800–2000: Views from Geography and History*. Boston: Kluwer Academic.

Kolossov, V. 2005. Border Studies: Changing Perspectives and Theoretical Approaches. *Geopolitics* 10:606–632.

Kolossov, V., and O'Loughlin, J. 1998. New Borders for New World Orders: Territorialities at the Fin-de-siecle. *GeoJournal* 44 (3): 259–273.

Konrad, V., and Nicol, H. 2008. *Beyond Walls: Reinventing the Canada-United States Borderlands*. Aldershot: Ashgate.

Koscher, K., Juels, A., Brajkovic, V., and Kohno, T. 2009. EPC RFID Tag Security Weaknesses and Defenses: Passport Cards, Enhanced Drivers Licenses, and Beyond. *Proceedings of the 16th ACM Conference on Computer and Communications Security*: 33–42.

Kramsch, O. 2001. Towards Cosmopolitan Governance? Prospects and Possibilities for the Maas-Rhein Euregio. In G. Bucken-Knapp and M. Schack, eds., *Borders Matter*. Aabenraa: IFG. Pp. 173–192.

———. 2002a. Re-Imagining the Scalar Topologies of Cross-Border Governance: Eu(ro)regions in the Postcolonial Present. *Space and Polity* 6 (2): 169–196.

———. 2002b. Navigating the Spaces of Kantian Reason: Notes on Cosmopolitical Governance within the Cross-Border Euregios of the European Union. *Geopolitics* 6 (2): 27–50.

———. 2003. Re-imagining the "Scalar Fix" of Transborder Governance: The Case of the Maas-Rhein Euregio. In E. Berg and H. van Houtum, eds., *Routing Borders between Territories, Discourses and Practices*. London: Ashgate. Pp. 220–228.

———. 2007. Querying Cosmopolis at the Borders of Europe. *Environment and Planning A* 39:1582–1600.

Kramsch, O., and Hooper, B., eds. 2004. *Cross-Border Governance in the European Union*. London: Routledge.

Kratochwil, F. 1986. Of Systems, Boundaries and Territoriality: An Inquiry into the Formation of the State System. *World Politics* 39 (1): 21–52.

Kristof, L. 1959. The Nature of Frontiers and Boundaries. *Annals of the Association of American Geographers* 49:269–282.

Kyoto Protocol to the United Nations Framework Convention on Climate Change. 1998. *United Nations*. Available at http://unfccc.int/resource/docs/convkp/kpeng.pdf.

Lahav, G. 2004. *Immigration and Politics in the New Europe: Reinventing Borders*. Cambridge: Cambridge University Press.

Lahav, G., and Guiraudon, V. 2000. Comparative Perspectives on Border Control: Away from the Border and Outside the State. In P. Andreas and T. Snyder, eds., *The Wall around the West*. Lanham, MD: Rowman & Littlefield. Pp. 55–77.

Lefebvre, H. 1991. *The Production of Space*. Oxford: Blackwell.

Le Gales, P. 1998. Government and Governance of Regions. In P. Le Gales and C. Lequesne, eds., *Regions in Europe*. London: Routledge. Pp. 239–269.

Le Gales, P., and Lequesne, C., eds. 1998. *Regions in Europe*. London: Routledge.

Leitner, H., and Ehrkamp, P. 2006. Transnationalism and Migrants' Imaginings of Citizenship. *Environment and Planning A* 38:1615–1632.

Leresche, J. P., and Saez, G. 2002. Political Frontier Regimes: Towards Cross-Border Governance? In M. Perkmann and N.-L. Sum, eds., *Globalisation, Regionalization and Cross-Border Regions*. London: Palgrave. Pp. 77–99.

Liersch, I. 2009. Electronic Passports—From Secure Specifications to Secure Implementations. *Information Security Technical Report* 14:96–100.

Lipschutz, R. 1995. On Security. In R. Lipschutz, ed., *On Security*. New York: Columbia University Press. Pp. 1–23.

Lodge, J., ed. 2007. *Are You Who You Say You Are? The EU and Biometric Borders*. Nijmegen: Wolf Legal Publishers.

Longan, M., and Purcell, D. 2011. Engineering Community and Place: Facebook as Megaengineering. In S. Brun, ed., *Engineering Earth*. Dordrecht: Springer.

Lyon, D. 2005. The Border Is Everywhere: ID Cards, Surveillance and the Other. In E. Zureik and M. Salter, eds., *Global Surveillance and Policing*. Cullompton: Willan. Pp. 66–82.

———. 2007a. *Surveillance Studies: An Overview* . Cambridge: Polity Press.

———. 2007b. Surveillance, Security and Social Sorting: Emerging Research Priorities. *International Criminal Justice Review* 17 (3): 161–170.

———. 2008. Biometrics, Identification and Surveillance. *Bioethics* 22 (9): 499–508.

Macartney, J. 2006. Dissident Jailed "After Yahoo Handed Evidence to Police." *The Times*, February 10.

Machado, L. O., Novaes, A. R., and Monteiro, L. do R. 2009. Building Walls, Breaking Barriers: Territory, Integration and the Rule of Law in Frontier Zones. *Journal of Borderlands Studies* 24 (3): 97–114.

MacLeod, G., and Jones, M. 2001. Renewing the Geography of Regions. *Environment and Planning D* 19 (6): 669–695.

Mann, M. 1984. The Autonomous Power of the State. *European Journal of Sociology* 25:185–213.

Marks, G. 1996. An Actor-Centered Approach to Multi-Level Governance. *Regional and Federal Studies* 6 (2): 20–40.

Marks, K. 2006. Rising Tide of Global Warming Threatens Pacific Island States. *The Independent*, 25 October.

Martinez, O. J. 1994. *Border People: Life and Society in the U.S.-Mexico Borderlands*. Tucson: University of Arizona Press.

Marty, D. 2006. *Alleged Secret Detentions and Unlawful Inter-state Transfers of Detainees Involving Council of Europe Member States*. Report, Committee on Legal Affairs and Human Rights, Council of Europe, June 12.

Maurer, B. 2008. Re-Regulating Offshore Finance? *Geography Compass* 2 (1): 155–175.

McGirk, T. 2009. Could Israelis Face War Crimes Charges over Gaza? *Time*, January 23.

Meserve, J., and Ahlers, M. 2007. Canadian Firetruck Responding to U.S. Call Held up at Border. CNN, November 14. Available at http://edition.cnn .com/2007/US/11/14/border.firetruck.

Michaelsen, S., and Johnson, D., eds. 1997. *Border Theory: The Limits of Cultural Politics*. Minneapolis: University of Minnesota Press.

Minghi, J. V. 1963/1969. Boundary Studies in Political Geography. In R. E. Kasperson and J. V. Minghi, eds., *The Structure of Political Geography*. Chicago: Aldine. Pp. 140–160.

———. 1991. From Conflict to Harmony in Border Landscapes. In D. Rumley and J. Minghi, eds., *The Geography of Border Landscapes*. London: Routledge. Pp. 15–30.

Mojtahed-Zadeh, P. 2006. "Boundary" in Ancient Persian Tradition of Statehood: An Introduction to the Origins of the Concept of Boundary in Pre-modern History. *GeoJournal* 66 (4): 273–283.

Morehouse, B. 2004. Theoretical Approaches to Border Spaces and Identities. In V. Pavlakovich-Kochi, B. Morehouse, and D. Wastl-Walter, eds., *Challenged Borderlands*. Aldershot: Ashgate. Pp. 19–39.

Mountz, A. 2011. The Enforcement Archipelago: Detention, Haunting, and Asylum on Islands. *Political Geography*, doi:10.1016/j.polgeo.2011.01.005.

Muller, B. 2008. Securing the Political Imagination: Popular Culture, the Security Dispositif, and the Biometric State. *Security Dialogue* 39 (2/3): 199–220.

Murphy A. 1993. Emerging Local Linkages within the European Community: Challenging the Dominance of the State. *Tijdschrift voor Economische en Sociale Geografie* 84:103–118.

———. 1996. The Sovereign State System as Political-Territorial Ideal: Historical and Contemporary Considerations. In T. J. Biersteker and C. Weber, eds., *State Sovereignty as Social Construct*. Cambridge: Cambridge University Press. Pp. 81–120.

———. 1999. International Law and the Sovereign State: Challenges to the Status Quo. In G. J. Demko and W. B. Wood, eds., *Reordering the World*. Boulder, CO: Westview. Pp. 227–245.

Murphy, S. D. 1996. *Humanitarian Intervention: The United Nations in an Evolving World Order*. Philadelphia: University of Pennsylvania Press.

Nevins, J. 2002. *The Rise of the "Illegal Alien" and the Remaking of the U.S.-Mexico Boundary*. New York: Routledge.

Newman, D., ed. 1999. *Boundaries, Territory and Postmodernity*. London: Frank Cass.

———. 2003. Boundaries. In J. Agnew, K. Mitchell, and G. Toal, eds., *A Companion to Political Geography*. Oxford: Blackwell. Pp. 123–137.

———. 2006a. The Lines That Continue to Separate Us: Borders in Our "Borderless" World. *Progress in Human Geography* 30 (2): 143–161.

———. 2006b. Borders and Bordering: Towards an Interdisciplinary Dialogue. *European Journal of Social Theory* 9 (2): 171–186.

Newman, D., and Paasi, A. 1998. Fences and Neighbours in the Postmodern World: Boundary Narratives in Political Geography. *Progress in Human Geography* 22 (2): 186–207.

Nicol, H., and Townsend-Gault, I., eds. 2005. *Holding the Line: Borders in a Global World*. Vancouver: University of British Columbia Press.

Norman, E., and Bakker, K. 2009. Transgressing Scales: Transboundary Water Governance between Canada and the US. *Annals of the Association of American Geographers* 99 (1): 99–117.

O'Brian, R. 1992. *Global Financial Integration: The End of Geography*. New York: Council on Foreign Relations Press.

O'Dowd, L. 2002a. Transnational Integration and Cross-Border Regions in the European Union. In J. Anderson, ed., *Transnational Democracy*. London: Routledge. Pp. 111–128.

———. 2002b. The Changing Significance of European Borders. *Regional and Federal Studies* 12 (4): 13–36.

O'Dowd, L., and Wilson, T., eds. 1996. *Borders, Nations and States*. Aldershot: Avebury.

Ohmae, K. 1990. *The Borderless World: Power and Strategy in the Interlinked Economy*. London: Collins.

O'Lear, S. 2010. *Environmental Politics: Scale and Power*. Cambridge: Cambridge University Press.

Paasi, A. 1996. *Territories, Boundaries and Consciousness: The Changing Geographies of the Finnish-Russian Border*. Chichester: Wiley.

———. 1999. Boundaries as Social Processes: Territoriality in the World of Flows. In D. Newman, ed., *Boundaries, Territory and Postmodernity*. London: Frank Cass. Pp. 69–89.

———. 2002. Place and Region: Regional Worlds and Words. *Progress in Human Geography* 26 (6): 802–811.

———. 2003a. Region and Place: Regional Identity in Question. *Progress in Human Geography* 27 (4): 475–485.

———. 2003b. Territory. In J. Agnew, K. Mitchell, and G. Toal, eds., *A Companion to Political Geography*. Oxford: Blackwell. Pp. 109–120.

———. 2005. The Changing Discourses on Political Boundaries: Mapping the Backgrounds, Contexts and Contents. In H. van Houtum, O. Kramsch, and W. Zierhofer, eds., *B/ordering the World*. London: Ashgate. Pp. 17–31.

———. 2009. Bounded Spaces in a "Borderless World": Border Studies, Power and the Anatomy of Territory. *Journal of Power* 2 (2): 213–234.

Paasi, A., and Prokkola, E.-K. 2008. Territorial Dynamics, Cross-Border Work and Everyday Life in the Finnish-Swedish Border Area. *Space & Polity* 12 (1): 13–29.

Painter J. 2002. Multilevel Citizenship, Identity and Regions in Contemporary Europe. In J. Anderson, ed., *Transnational Democracy*. London: Routledge. Pp. 93–110.

Palan, R. 2006. *The Offshore World: Sovereign Markets, Virtual Places, and Nomad Millionaires*. Ithaca, NY: Cornell University Press.

Pavlakovich-Kochi, V., Morehouse, B., and Wastl-Walter, D., eds. 2004. *Challenged Borderlands: Transcending Political and Cultural Boundaries*. Ashgate: Aldershot.

Payan, T., and Vasquez, A. 2007. The Costs of Homeland Security. In E. Brunet-Jailly, ed., *Borderlands*. Ottawa: University of Ottawa Press. Pp. 231–258.

Pellow, D., ed. 1996. *Setting Boundaries: The Anthropology of Spatial and Social Organization*. London: Bergin & Gravey.

Perkmann, M. 1999. Building Governance Institutions across European Borders. *Regional Studies* 33 (7): 657–667.

———. 2002. Euroregions: Institutional Entrepreneurship in the European Union. In M. Perkmann and N.-L. Sum, eds., *Globalization, Regionalization, and Cross-Border Regions*. Basingstoke: Palgrave. Pp. 103–124.

———. 2003. Cross-Border Regions in Europe: Significance and Drivers of Regional Cross-Border Cooperation. *European Regional Studies* 10 (2): 153–171.

———. 2007a. Construction of New Territorial Scales: A Framework and Case Study of the EUREGIO Cross-Border Region. *Regional Studies* 41 (2): 253–266.

———. 2007b. Policy Entrepreneurship and Multilevel Governance: A Comparative Study of European Cross-Border Regions. *Environment and Planning C* 25:861–879.

Perkmann, M., and Sum, N. L. 2002. Globalization, Regionalization, and Cross Border Regions: Scales, Discourses and Governance. In M. Perkmann and N.-L. Sum, eds., *Globalization, Regionalization, and Cross-Border Regions*. London: Palgrave. Pp. 3–24.

Pickering, S. 2006. Border Narratives: From Talking to Performing Borderlands. In S. Pickering and L. Weber, eds., *Borders, Mobility and Technologies of Control*. Dordrecht: Springer. Pp. 45–62.

Pohl, W. 2001. Conclusion: The Transformation of Frontiers. In W. Pohl, I. Wood, and H. Reimitz, eds., *The Transformation of Frontiers from Late Antiquity to the Carolingians*. Leiden: Brill. Pp. 247–260.

Popescu, G. 2008. The Conflicting Logics of Cross-Border Reterritorialization: Geopolitics of Euroregions in Eastern Europe. *Political Geography* 27 (4): 418–438.

———. 2011. Transcending the National Space: The Institutionalization of Cross-Border Territory in the Lower Danube Euroregion. In D. Wastl-Walter, ed., *Research Companion to Border Studies*. Pp. 607–624.

Prescott, J. R. V. 1965. *The Geography of Frontiers and Boundaries*. Chicago: Aldine.

———. 1987. *Political Frontiers and Boundaries*. London: Allen & Unwin.

Rabo, A. 2006. Trade across Borders: Views from Aleppo. In I. Brandell, ed., *State Frontiers: Borders and Boundaries in the Middle East*. London: I. B. Tauris. Pp. 53–74.

Ramos, J. 2007. Managing US-Mexico Transborder Co-operation on Local Security Issues and the Canadian Relationship. In E. Brunet-Jailly, ed., *Borderlands*. Ottawa: University of Ottawa Press. Pp. 259–276.

Ratzel, F. 1897. *Politische Geographie*. Munich: Oldenbourg.

Reynolds, P. 2007. Russia ahead in Arctic "Gold Rush." BBC News, August 1. Available at http://news.bbc.co.uk/2/hi/6925853.stm.

Rome Statute of the International Criminal Court. 1998. *United Nations*, Doc. A/CONF.183/9. Available at http://untreaty.un.org/cod/icc/statute/romefra.htm.

Ruggie, J. 1993. Territoriality and Beyond: Problematizing Modernity in International Relations. *International Organization* 47 (1): 139–174.

Rumford, C. 2006a. Theorizing Borders. *European Journal of Social Theory* 9 (2): 155–170.

———. 2006b. Rethinking European Spaces: Governance beyond Territoriality. *Comparative European Politics* 4 (2): 127–140.

———. 2007. Does Europe Have Cosmopolitan Borders? *Globalizations* 4 (3): 327–339.

———. 2008a. *Cosmopolitan Spaces: Globalization, Europe, Theory.* London: Routledge.

———. 2008b. Citizens and Borderwork in Europe. *Space and Polity* 12 (1): 1–12.

Rumley, D. R., and Minghi J., eds. 1991. *The Geography of Border Landscapes.* Routledge: London.

Sack, R. 1986. *Human Territoriality: Its Theory and History.* Cambridge: Cambridge University Press.

Sahlins, P. 1989. *Boundaries: The Making of France and Spain in the Pyrenees.* Berkeley: University of California Press.

Said, E. 1978. *Orientalism.* New York: Vintage.

Salter, M. 2003. *Rights of Passage: The Passport in International Relations.* Boulder, CO: Lynne Reinner.

———. 2004. Passports, Mobility, and Security: How Smart Can the Border Be? *International Studies Perspectives* 5:71–91.

———. 2006. The Global Visa Regime and the Political Technologies of the International Self. *Alternatives* 31:167–189.

Sassen, S. 1999. Embedding the Global in the National: Implications for the Role of the State. In A. D. Smith, D. J. Solinger, and S. C. Topik, eds., *States and Sovereignty in the Global Economy.* London: Routledge. Pp. 158–171.

———. 2001. *The Global City: New York, London, Tokyo.* Princeton, NJ: Princeton University Press.

———. 2006. *Territory, Authority, Rights: From Medieval to Global Assemblages.* Princeton, NJ: Princeton University Press.

Schulz, M., Soderbaum, F., and Ojendal, J., eds. 2001. *Regionalization in a Globalizing World.* London: Zed Books.

Scott, J. W. 1999. European and North American Contexts for Cross-Border Regionalism. *Regional Studies* 33 (7): 605–617.

———. 2000. Transboundary Cooperation on Germany's Borders: Strategic Regionalism through Multilevel Governance. *Journal of Borderland Studies* 15 (1): 143–167.

———. 2002. On the Political Economy of Cross-Border Regionalism: Regional Development and Co-operation on the US-Mexican Border. In M. Perkmann and N.-L. Sum, eds., *Globalization, Regionalization, and Cross-Border Regions.* London: Palgrave. Pp. 191–211.

Shapiro, M. J., and Alker, H., eds. 1996. *Challenging Boundaries: Global Flows, Territorial Identities.* Minneapolis: University of Minnesota Press.

Sheller, M., and Urry, J. 2006. The New Mobilities Paradigm. *Environment and Planning A* 38:207–226.

Sidaway, J. 2001. Rebuilding Bridges: A Critical Geopolitics of Iberian Transfrontier Cooperation in a European Context. *Environment and Planning D* 19:743–778.

Smith, B. 1995. On Drawing Lines on a Map. In A. U. Frank, W. Kuhn, and D. M. Mark, eds., *Spatial Information Theory: Proceedings of COSIT '95.* Berlin: Springer Verlag. Pp. 475–484.

Soderbaum, F., and Taylor, I., eds. 2008. *Afro-Regions: The Dynamics of Cross-Border Micro-Regionalism in Africa.* Stockholm: Nordic African Institute.

Sohn, C., Reitel, B., and Walther, O. 2009. Cross-Border Metropolitan Integration in Europe: The Case of Luxembourg, Basel and Geneva, *Environment and Planning C* 27:922–939.

Soja, E. 1971. *The Political Organization of Space.* Washington, DC: Association of American Geographers.

Sparke, M. 2002a. Between Post-Colonialism and Cross-Border Regionalism. *Space and Polity* 6 (2): 203–213.

———. 2002b. Not a State, But More than a State of Mind: Cascadia and the Geo-Economics of Cross-Border Regionalism. In M. Perkmann and N.-L. Sum, eds., *Globalization, Regionalization, and Cross-Border Regions.* London: Palgrave. Pp. 212–238.

———. 2004. Passports into Credit Cards: On the Borders and Spaces of Neoliberal Citizenship. In J. Migdal, ed., *Boundaries and Belonging.* Cambridge: Cambridge University Press. Pp. 251–283.

———. 2005. *In the Space of Theory: Postfoundational Geographies of the Nation-State.* Minneapolis: University of Minnesota Press.

———. 2006. A Neoliberal Nexus: Economy, Security and the Biopolitics of Citizenship on the Border. *Political Geography* 25 (2): 151–180.

Sparke, M., Sidaway, J., Bunnell, T., and Grundy-Warr, C. 2004. Triangulating the Borderless World: Geographies of Power in the Indonesia-Malaysia-Singapore Growth Triangle. *Transactions of the Institute of British Geographers* 29 (4): 485–498.

Steinberg, P. 2010. You Are (Not) Here: On the Ambiguity of Flag Planting and Finger Pointing in the Arctic. *Political Geography* 29:81–84.

Storey, D. 2001. *Territory: The Claiming of Space.* Harlow: Prentice Hall.

Storper, M. 1995. The Resurgence of Regional Economies Ten Years Later: The Region as a Nexus of Untraded Interdependencies. *European Urban and Regional Studies* 2/3:191–221.

———. 1997. *The Regional World: Territorial Development in a Global Economy.* London: Guilford Press.

Strüver, A. 2003. Presenting Representations: On the Analysis of Narratives and Images along the Dutch-German Border. In E. Berg and H. van Houtum, eds., *Routing Borders between Territories, Discourses and Practices.* Aldershot: Ashgate. Pp. 161–176.

Sullivan, E. 2009. Napolitano Concedes Airline Security System Failed. Associated Press, December 28.

Sum, N.-L. 2002. Globalization, Regionalization and Cross-Border Modes of Growth in East Asia: The (Re-)Constitution of "Time-Space Governance." In M. Perkmann and N.-L. Sum, eds., *Globalization, Regionalization, and Cross-Border Regions.* London: Palgrave. Pp. 50–76.

Swyngedouw, E. 1997. Neither Global nor Local: "Glocalisation" and the Politics of Scale. In K. Cox, ed., *Spaces of Globalization.* New York: Guilford. Pp. 137–166.

Taylor, P. 1994. The State as Container: Territoriality in the Modern World-System. *Progress in Human Geography* 18:51–162.

———. 1995. Beyond Containers: Internationality, Interstateness, Interterritoriality. *Progress in Human Geography* 19 (1): 1–15.

Taylor, P., and Flint, C. 2000. *Political Geography, World-Economy, Nation-State and Locality.* Harlow: Pearson.

Telò, M. 2001. Globalization, New Regionalism and the Role of the European Union. In M. Telò, ed., *European Union and New Regionalism*. Ashgate: Aldershot. Pp. 1–20.

Terriff, T., Croft, S., James, L., and Morgan, P. 1999. *Security Studies Today*. Cambridge: Polity Press.

Thrift, N. 1983. On the Determination of Social Action in Space and Time. *Environment and Planning D* 1 (1): 23–57.

———. 1990. For a New Regional Geography 1. *Progress in Human Geography* 14:272–279.

———. 1991. For a New Regional Geography 2. *Progress in Human Geography* 15:456–465.

———. 1993. For a New Regional Geography 3. *Progress in Human Geography* 17:92–100.

Toal (O'Tuathail), G. 1996. *Critical Geopolitics: The Politics of Writing Global Space*. Minneapolis: University of Minnesota Press.

———. 1998. Political Geography III: Dealing with Deterritorialization. *Progress in Human Geography* 22 (1): 81–93.

———. 1999. De-Territorialised Threats and Global Dangers: Geopolitics and Risk Society. In D. Newman, ed., *Boundaries, Territory and Postmodernity*. London: Frank Cass. Pp. 17–32.

———. 2000. Borderless Worlds? Problematising Discourses of Deterritorialization. In N. Kliot and D. Newman, eds., *Geopolitics at the End of the Twentieth Century*. London: Frank Cass. Pp. 139–154.

Torpey, J. 2000. States and the Regulation of Migration in the Twentieth-Century North Atlantic World. In P. Andreas and T. Snyder, eds., *The Wall around the West*. Lanham, MD: Rowman & Littlefield. Pp. 31–54.

Tsoukala, A. 2008. Security, Risk and Human Rights: A Vanishing Relationship? Centre for European Policy Studies, Special Report. Brussels, September. Pp. 1–17. Available at http://www.ceps.eu/files/book/1703.pdf.

Tyner, J. 2005. *Iraq, Terror, and the Philippines' Will to War*. Lanham, MD: Rowman & Littlefield.

———. 2006. *Oriental Bodies: Discourse and Discipline in U.S. Immigration Policy, 1875–1942*. Lanham, MD: Lexington Books.

UK Border Agency. 2010. *How Do I Use IRIS to Enter the UK?* Available at http://www.ukba.homeoffice.gov.uk/travellingtotheuk/Enteringtheuk/usingiris/howenterwithiris.

United Nations Conference on Trade and Development. 2008. *Transnational Corporations and the Infrastructure Challenge*. World Investment Report. Available at http://www.unctad.org/en/docs/wir2008_en.pdf.

Urry, J. 2000. *Sociology beyond Societies: Mobilities for the Twenty-First Century*. London: Routledge.

van der Ploeg, I. 1999a. The Illegal Body: "Eurodac" and the Politics of Biometric Identification. *Ethics and Information Technology* 1 (4): 295–302.

———. 1999b. Written on the Body: Biometrics and Identity. *Computers and Society* 29 (1): 37–44.

van der Velde, M., and van Houtum, H. 2004. The Threshold of Indifference: Rethinking Immobility in Explaining Cross-Border Labour Mobility. *Review of Regional Research* 24 (1): 39–49.

van Houtum, H. 2002. Borders of Comfort: Spatial Economic Bordering Processes in the European Union. *Regional and Federal Studies* 12 (4): 37–58.

van Houtum, H., and Boedeltje, F. 2009. Europe's Shame: Death at the Borders of the EU. *Antipode* 41 (2): 226–230.

van Houtum, H., Kramsch, O., and Ziefhofer, W. 2005. *B/ordering Space*. Aldershot: Ashgate.

van Houtum, H., and Strüver, A. 2002. Borders, Strangers, Doors and Bridges. *Space and Polity* 6 (2): 141–146.

van Houtum, H., and van Naerssen, T. 2002. Bordering, Ordering and Othering. *Tijdschrift voor Economische en Sociale Geografie* 93:125–136.

Vaughan-Williams, N. 2008. Borderwork beyond Inside/Outside? Frontex, the Citizen-Detective and the War on Terror. *Space and Polity* 12 (1): 63–79.

Vincent, A. 1987. *Theories of the State*. Oxford: Blackwell.

Waever, O. 1993. Societal Security: The Concept. In O. Waever, B. Buzan, M. Kelstrup, and P. Lemaitre, eds., *Identity, Migration and the New Security Agenda in Europe*. London: Pinter. Pp. 17–40.

Walker, R. B. J. 1993. *Inside/Outside: International Relations as Political Theory*. Cambridge: Cambridge University Press.

Wallerstein, I. 1999. States? Sovereignty? The Dilemmas of Capitalists in an Age of Transition. In A. D. Smith, D. J. Solinger, and S. C. Topik, eds., *States and Sovereignty in the Global Economy*. London: Routledge. Pp. 20–33.

Walters, W. 2002. Mapping Schengenland: Denaturalizing the Border. *Environment and Planning D* 20:561–580.

———. 2004. The Frontiers of the European Union: A Geostrategic Perspective. *Geopolitics* 9 (2): 674–698.

———. 2006a. Rethinking Borders beyond the State. *Comparative European Politics* 4 (2/3): 141–159.

———. 2006b. Border/Control. *European Journal of Social Theory* 9 (2): 187–204.

Warf, B. 1989. Telecommunications and the Globalization of Financial Services. *Professional Geographer* 31:257–271.

———. 2001. Segueways into Cyberspace: Multiple Geographies of the Digital Divide. *Environment and Planning B* 28:3–19.

———. 2002. Tailored for Panama: Offshore Banking at the Crossroads of the Americas. *Geografiska Annaler B* 84 (1): 47–61.

———. 2008. *Time-Space Compression: Historical Geographies*. London: Routledge.

———. 2010. Geographies of Global Internet Censorship. *GeoJournal* 76 (1): 1–23.

Warf, B., and Purcell, D. 2001. The Currency of Currency: Electronic Money, Electronic Spaces. In T. Leinbach and S. Brunn, eds., *The Worlds of Electronic Commerce*. London: Wiley. Pp. 223–240.

Watts, M. 2007. Revolutionary Islam. In D. Gregory and A. Pred, eds., *Violent Geographies*. New York: Routledge. Pp. 175–204.

Whittaker, C. R. 1994. *Frontiers of the Roman Empire: A Social and Economic Study*. Baltimore, MD: Johns Hopkins University Press.

Williams, J. 2003. Territorial Borders, International Ethics and Geography: Do Good Fences Still Make Good Neighbors? *Geopolitics* 8 (2): 25–46.

Wonders, N. 2006. Global Flows, Semi-permeable Borders and New Channels of Inequality. In S. Pickering and L. Weber, eds., *Borders, Mobility and Technologies of Control*. Dordrecht: Springer. Pp. 63–86.

Wong-Gonzales, P. 2004. Conflict and Accommodation in the Arizona-Sonora Region. In V. Pavlakovich-Kochi, B. Morehouse, and D. Wastl-Walter, eds., *Challenged Borderlands*. Aldershot: Ashgate. Pp. 123–154.

Yoder, J. 2003. Bridging the European Union and Eastern Europe: Cross-Border Cooperation and the Euroregions. *Regional and Federal Studies* 13 (3): 90–106.

Index

About the Author

Gabriel Popescu is assistant professor of political geography in the Department of Political Science at Indiana University, South Bend. He holds BA and MA degrees in geography from the University of Bucharest, Romania, as well as MA and PhD degrees in geography from Kent State University and Florida State University, respectively. His academic interests include geopolitics, social theory, border studies, regionalism, ethnicity, and diaspora. His scholarship is located at the intersection of power, territory, identity, and transnationalism and focuses on the changes taking place in the spatial organization of social life under globalization. His recent work has appeared in *Geopolitics*, *Political Geography*, and several edited volumes.